GOOD GIRLS DO

Sex Chronicles of a Shameless Generation

SIMONA CHIOSE

ECW Press

NATIONAL LIBRARY OF CANADA CATALOGUING IN PUBLICATION DATA

Chiose, Simona
Good girls do: sex chronicles of a shameless generation

ISBN 1-55022-423-9

1. Sex I. Title.

HQ21.C515 2001 306.7 C00-933263-4

Cover and text design by Tania Craan
Cover photo by Rowan Seddon-Harvey/ Photonica
Layout by Mary Bowness

Printed by Transcon

Distributed in Canada by General Distribution Services,
325 Humber College Blvd., Toronto, ON, M9W 7C3

Distributed in the United States by LPC Group
1436 West Randolph St., Chicago. IL 60607, U.S.A.

Published by ECW PRESS
2120 Queen Street East, Suite 200, Toronto, ON M4E 1E2
ecwpress.com

This book is set in Avenir and Garamond.

PRINTED AND BOUND IN CANADA

The publication of *Good Girls Do* has been generously supported by the Canada Council, the Ontario Arts Council and the Government of Canada through the Book Publishing Industry Development Program. Canadä

For my parents

Acknowledgements

Thanks to Jack David for asking me to write a book in the first place and then agreeing, a year later, that it would be all right if it wasn't about the Coen brothers. To my editor, Michael Holmes, for getting it so quickly and conveying what he didn't get so sensitively. Thanks and good luck to Jack David's Centennial College book publishing class, for their comments, questions and interest. For the enthusiasm that turned an idea into a book, Moe Berg, and for being an inspiring partner in crime, Roxane Ward. To anyone who thinks they recognize themselves here: you're right, it's you, so thank you. The many people I interviewed and who shared with me their experiences, thoughts and feelings, in particular Alana and Victoria, all the women of the bathhouse of July 1999 and James and Sara — I hope you see yourselves, at least a bit. Years of thanks go to my friends, John Hodgins and Rachel Shain, for staying around when some of the things that happen to me in this book were driving them crazy and also for telling me what to leave out. And to Paul Fairweather, thank you for your black pen across these pages, but also for all the things you don't want to be thanked for but which made my writing of this book part of a much better life.

CHAPTER **ONE**

MOTHERS AND DAUGHTERS

The phone rang on a Thursday night in late summer. The call display told me it was my mother. She'd already left two messages that day and I knew from her clipped tone what they were about.

That day, *The Globe and Mail*, known as Canada's national newspaper, had published a column of mine where I said that horror movies turned me on. The argument wasn't terribly sophisticated: my fear thrilled me and made me want to cuddle and from there. . . . It was light, it was breezy; I'd hoped it was funny. It also said, in print, that I had had sex. Not wild, orgiastic sex at all-night coke and heroin-fueled parties that are every parent's nightmare — just sex with boyfriends. Nothing too radical there, surely nothing which could offend my mother.

It was the second time in less than a week that I'd written about sex, and the fifth time in less than a month that my name had come up in connection with the subject in a daily paper. There was an article about me going to strip clubs with other women. There was a chronicle about a lesbian bathhouse I attended. There was a book review I had written on books about women having sex. There was a gossip item about being one of the women in a photograph on the front cover of a small literary journal that most people had never heard of until its publisher decided to put out a "Literary Babes" issue. Most of this was research for this book and the research had put me in touch with people I would have never met otherwise, but for my parents each "incident" (for they were all "incidents") had provoked a crisis and an avalanche of phone calls. By the time we slammed the phone down, usually simultaneously, I would be lying on my kitchen floor, simmering in a pool of sweat and blowing smoke rings into the fine mist of heat and humidity that filled my apartment every day. The heat and the fevered debates were slowly melting me down. I was sure I was acquiring an ulcer.

Maybe a belief in miracles isn't such a bad thing to cultivate. Maybe this time the sparring could be noble, civil, and non-partisan, and we could enjoy the sport for its own pleasures. I picked up.

"I want you to explain to me what your story is about," were my mother's first words.

"It's not true. None of it is true. I made it up," were mine. When in doubt, lie. Anyway, I wasn't entirely sure how much I had exaggerated in the writing. The more colorful details perhaps. Don't they call it literary journalism?

"I don't care if it's true. I don't care what you do. I don't want you to tell me it's not true. I want to know why your name is on top of the story," she said.

"Mmm. 'Cause I wrote it?"

"How could you?"

I slouched onto the tiles and watched the blood begin to flow.

My father, she said, had spent the early evening lying on the sofa vocalizing on how I was ruining my life. She had spent her workday afternoon apologizing for the sins of her daughter to one of her work colleagues, someone who had read the column and had asked whether we were related. "Wow, someone read my story," I said. "Cool."

"That's the kind of story you want to be known for?" she retorted.

"Isn't it better to be infamous than unknown?" said I, nicely reverting to philosophical teenage brattiness.

"Anyway, it's not my problem if your friends don't like what I write. Why don't you say you don't know me?" Sometimes I wonder why adults agree to grow up when adolescents get away with so much more smart-aleck behavior.

Her point, the same one she'd made the other four times that month, was that a woman of my advancing age (29) should keep her sexual life private. Sexuality in general was a matter between two people, not something to broadcast in a national paper, no matter how general the details. And most importantly, no self-respecting woman was writing about sex.

"If you want . . ."

I knew the end of that sentence. If I wanted "a good life, with a nice husband, children," I should stop writing about sex. I wanted to point out that in the past week I'd read articles written by women on anal sex, on bondage, on actually being strippers, not on going to see strippers. Instead I said,

"Don't give me the talk you didn't give me 15 years ago," not entirely sure what I meant.

"Well, I told you then. They are looking at you as someone who'll write about sex. No one else will do it." ("They" were the paper's editors.) She obviously didn't know what I meant either, but a good fighter is not stopped by a *non sequitur.*

"Good. That means I can pay my rent."

"You are carving out a niche as a woman who'll say anything about herself just to get attention," my mother screamed into the phone. All I could think was that as far as I could tell from my bank balance, I hardly had any niche market cornered.

"Look, when men do the same no one says anything. Why doesn't that offend you?" I asked her.

"Because you're my daughter. And also, you're not a man, you're a woman."

I lost my patience.

"Oh, for God's sake. All it says is that I'm not a virgin. I'm not saying anything," I told her, then added, "I thought it made some interesting points." At that moment, though, I would have been hard-pressed to figure out what they were and was woefully sorry I'd written the column. Why did I have to work sex into something about horror movies? Why hadn't I come up with a more erudite idea, the sexual politics of vampire films even? My mother knows my weaknesses.

"Madelaine Albright and that woman, that woman, what's her name, on CNN?"

"Christiane Amanpour," I said, sighing. Christiane Amanpour, the woman who reported as a freelancer from every war-torn zone in the world, was a stringer from the Gulf War, never wore a shred of make-up, could speak five or six languages, and had just married a very cute White House press officer. Christiane Amanpour: not a few of my female friends wished we'd grow up to be her.

"Is that her name? Well, her. She never wrote anything like that."

"How do you know?" We both knew she hadn't and even if she had her dirty prose was as well hidden as a dirty picture. Christiane Amanpour was probably writing Middle East political history at the age of 14; I was reading *Anna Karenina* and *Lady Chatterley's Lover* and wondering when any of the things in these books would happen to me and if they would be as fantastic as all that. Fated to frivolity.

I had been knocked out so the tone turned somewhat amiable. My mother and I went on for a while, having a semi-lucid conversation about women and writing and careers in between her admonishments for me to go to law school. Phones were eventually slammed because otherwise how can you end a conversation, but I can't stop wondering if she's right. After all, every mother worth her title must be able to evoke shame in her daughter.

CHAPTER TWO

WHAT A WONDERFUL WORLD

I wrote my first love letter at the age of six, folded it, and addressed it to a boy two years older than me. All it said was "I love you." I gave the note to his friend to give to him. Of course, the whole neighborhood found out and although this boy and I spent lots of time biking around the park in front of the apartment building where we both lived, he never kissed me. Instead, when he turned twelve, he kissed my best friend. She was the same age as him, had grown breasts, and had also taken to carrying a knife strapped to the inside of her boot.

The whole experience taught me one lesson: if I wanted future boys to kiss *me* and not my best friends, I'd better learn how to be as "bad" as my girlfriends were. My teenage years were spent wanting and failing to be the girl everyone gossiped about. I hardly even noticed how nasty such rumors were. All I knew was that these girls seemed to be having a great time. They wore make-up, lied to their boyfriends (they were always multiple) about going out with their girlfriends, and went to parties every weekend. Meanwhile, I was a virgin. The closest I got to attaining their status was to make these girls my best friends once again. They lent me their black mini-skirts and their blue and brown eye shadows and told me what jerks all the boyfriends were and how they were cheating around and which one should they dump? A few times, they tried to set me up with the jerks' friends. Occasionally these set-ups ended in a fumbling make-out session. Then I'd start talking, putting an end to the possibility of sexual initiation.

The first boy I ever truly wanted to kiss was as good at talking as kissing, which is why when his mother forbade me from seeing him anymore — "What are you doing?" she said. "You go to university. What do you want? Why are you here? He dropped out in grade nine!" — I almost flunked out of my first year of university. I was too busy writing him tearful letters I never sent instead of writing essays on proportional representation. In retrospect, the woman had my best interests in mind and had clearly been around too long to go along with my conceit that I was the solution to her son's problems.

The decade since has been spent trying to figure out how to be the "good girl" I am — someone who can't have sex without being emotionally involved — and also the "bad girl" I can be. I think I've made some strides toward not feeling guilty about being bad, not feeling guilty about what turns me on or how quickly it does so, or scared of the waves of desire I experience for those who have made me feel happy, physically elated, and loved.

It's been a funny time to learn how to grow up as a woman. We have myriad sexual possibilities. We can do and be anything we want; not just because as in the sixties and seventies the Pill is our birthright, but also because everywhere you look sex has long given up the missionary position. As long as they promise the possibility of bringing pleasure and happiness, we recognize and encourage all kinds of sexuality, from the polyamorous family to the S/M top-bottom couple. You can even opt out altogether and lay claim to perhaps the trendiest sexuality of all: celibacy.

(Celibacy seems guaranteed to me to induce constant thoughts of sex in those who master it.)

For most of us, though, being sexual involves having sex. With the explosion of the sex industry into the mainstream, being sexually satisfied is tantamount to being sexy and being sexy is less about the self and much more about being *au courant* with the latest sex fads or the recent habits of mega porn stars. How many women living in Canada, where the opportunity to bare almost all comes around for two months a year, are really keen on getting a Brazilian wax job? Yet women are heading to the torture table at the local beauty salon to rip it all off even though their livelihood does not depend on showing off their childlike nether regions. Just a decade ago, conservatives (and not a small number of liberals) would have fulminated against such loosening of public morals. Now the Christian Right and George W. Bush may try to tame Hollywood and abortion-rights groups and anything that smacks of sex, but in the malls of North America, the arena where everything is ultimately judged, anything goes. The exact fix to get someone off has never been so cheap or so easily available.

Some studies would suggest the majority of people do not practise anything that could really be classified as kinky. But if these non-believers were to explore and indulge, they would feel no shame. Sex was once something that men wanted and women were taught to withhold. Most women have no interest in being tamed like that anymore. In the place of those old rules, we are trying to make up new ones. But in the marketplace of pleasure new boundaries are just castles in the sand.

Next to an old apartment I was living in there is a leather store catering to bikers. On the first floor you can buy leather pants, skirts, shirts, belts with huge silver buckles, motorcycle pants, and for $39.95, an imitation human skull. (The real thing will cost you $1,500.) Walk to the back of the store, past the display cases of imitation biker gang rings and the racks of cowboy hats and leather chaps. A sign written in bright red magic marker arrests you. "If you are under 18 go no further."

Around the corner a narrow staircase leads to the basement. Compared to the cacophony of merchandise upstairs, the downstairs is spartan. A glass case circles the room. In the case rest various implements of sado-masochism accompanied by articles and photos of people using the implements. What the store obviously considers its *pièce de résistance* dominates the entirety of one wall. On a long, leather bench rests a dummy dressed as a gimp in black leather, a harness hanging over the whole contraption.

If you just walk by the store, you would never know what they have in the basement. A few might still find its wares offensive: the makeshift S/M museum certainly has more power to shock than the *Hustler* superstore in Los Angeles. This small neighborhood find is one of the last bastions of an old morality where private peccadilloes remained just that, private. The very same objects it has placed away from the eyes of every passer-by can be found in modern, glossy form in any number of clean, antiseptic, friendly, and supportive sex toy stores and in action in many XXX videos available at upscale adult video stores catering not to men in trench coats but to couples looking for a spicy date.

We're not giving up much by loosening our sexual mores. Or are we? Does losing the thrill of the forbidden, the suggestion, and the flirtation count as a loss? Does knowing the feel of leather that's been used against your body count as a loss?

Some years ago, a man lent me a copy of Sallie Tisdale's *Talk Dirty to Me*. The book was protected in a case with an indigo photograph of a hand offering an apple on its black cover. Shortly afterward, we had a dalliance, then a friendship which every once in a while flamed into a series of other dalliances. Part of the reason we became involved (for me) is because in the act of lending the book he seemed to be promising something. In my mental guide to boys, a guy who bought a book by an intellectual *Harper's* writer about sex, and by a woman to boot, had hidden depths just waiting to be discovered. Precisely the kind of imaginative promise guaranteed to lead to less than an ideal real-life situation.

Now, six years after Tisdale published her book, I doubt I would be swayed by the same gesture. Those sorts of romantic signals are passé. Giving a book as a seduction strategy seems as quaint as the owner of that leather store hiding the S/M tools in the basement. Even Tisdale's confessions are dated. We are no longer shocked by women writing about visiting adult video stores, learning to masturbate, or having fantasies about other women, as she did. Been there . . . Once Tisdale wrote shamelessly about the shape of her desires. More recently, she could be found writing on motherhood for the on-line magazine, *Salon*. Her impolite explorations of female sexuality have been replaced by polite (and, as usual, beautifully written) meditations on the joys and tribulations of motherhood.

Like an experienced, competent television anchor canned for a pretty young thing fresh out of journalism school, Tisdale's been replaced by younger, supposedly improved versions of herself: women who, if they've heard the word shame, have never thought of it in connection with themselves. Today, every fetish has an inalienable right not just to exist but also to be celebrated. Writing about sex now is more likely to run to stories about women dominating their boyfriends. Aside from wondering if the men ever mind having all their girlfriends' friends know their secrets, sometimes I don't want to know quite so much. We all agree that video killed the radio star, why not that explicit porn kills the imagination?

There are some restrictions. On the second season of *Ally McBeal*, Richard Fish, the smarmy lawyer who started the firm the show is set in, revealed two of his fetishes: he likes smelling shoes and he likes wattles. (A wattle is his term for the fold of skin older women develop under their chins.) On one episode, Fish's then girlfriend caught him touching then U.S. general attorney Janet Reno's wattle. All Fish was doing, he protested, was satisfying his need to touch wattles. He got dumped anyway. Moral of the episode: limit the expression of your fetishes to your beloved.

In the absence of a consenting partner, anyone can easily and anonymously get at least the representation of what they want over the Internet. A man in the 1920s would have had to procure a willing woman, rent a room, pay her up front, and then sneak back home. (Or he would have had to be wealthy enough to keep a mistress or two or three on call.) Unusual requests would have cost him extra and would have required some searching for a woman able to fulfill them.

The man himself may have momentarily felt ashamed that he was willing to spend money for such temporary relief, the same way Tisdale was ashamed at first to rent an explicit Swedish porn film. In the last couple of years, however, our hypothetical man would have had nothing to blush about. He could have investigated the topic of his choice on the Net — say girls and animals, to name one heavily advertised category — and slowly begin to think of himself as only a little bit outside of normal.

Legally, were he to act on his desires, he could still be thrown in jail. In the world of the Net, however, he is a consumer to be marketed to, admittedly perhaps one whose customer orders are a little more difficult, but for the right price hardly impossible, to fill. Should the world of pornography not already have produced your heart's desire, a growing number of companies are making to-order films using your scenario, words, props, characters. Make your own erotic adventure. As a consumer, our man gets respect. I signed up for several on-line adult sites during their many free promotional days. When canceling my subscription before they could charge my credit card, I was invariably greeted by an on-line survey or advertising page the Gap could easily adapt. Did I cancel my membership because the free offer was over, my card was used without authorization, had specific interests that were not met (could I specify what they were?) or because of a new partner? "We are sorry you did not find what you were looking for. Thank you for trying us out. May we recommend these other sites?" another exit ad asked me. No, thank *you*, I felt almost compelled to write back. I've never gotten that level of service in any other industry.

It's not just the Net that's made sex an ordinary commercial transaction. Brightly lit, clean adult video store chains cater to next door Tom and Sue with constantly sub-dividing categories, just so that they will find the precise physical act which drives both of them wild with desire. Seminars can then show Tom and Sue how to use the toys they saw in last night's flick. Should our couple grow tired of the same routine every night, they can head to a dungeon, or more conveniently and privately, hire a master or mistress from the back of any alternative North American weekly.

For the sex industry, the point is to keep Tom and Sue — or Sue and Alice, or Tom and Harry — buying stuff. For our couples, however, sooner or later each new entertainment grows tired and they have to upgrade to this year's fashions on the sex runways. First perhaps Sue decides that her Hitachi Magic Wand vibrator, available in bright Day-Glo colors and complete with all attachments, is really no more exciting than a porcelain dildo, the kind that may have been used on a Victorian woman. Then Tom decides that being whipped by a mistress in Sue's presence just doesn't do anything for him anymore. The sex industry knows this: the latest gizmos are called Dildonics, sexual toys that can be used over the Internet and manipulated by a remote user on you as you sit typing your reactions in the computer.

What everyone eventually discovers is that at most playing at sex can bring heightened sensations, that it can be fun, but like any game can get boring if played too often. Yesterday's taboo is just tomorrow's garage sale. Tom and Sue yearn to have their whole beings challenged, to have passion, sex and love blow their little world out of the water. "I still believe pleasure has to move and disturb,"[1] Regine Deforges says in an interview with Pauline Reage, the author of the scandalous (at the time) *Story of O* and surely that's what we're all looking for. How is a vibrator hooked up to your keyboard going to do that?

In 1954, Reage's tale of a woman who becomes a sex slave to please her lover was banned around the world. Even 15 years ago, when I bought it, it was hard to find in most bookstores. Now the local mega bookstore will carry ten copies of it in a bookcase-sized section of similar material and call it erotica.

A friend of mine borrowed my copy years ago, then, when she was short on cash, included it in a drop-off to the local used bookstore. Cheap thrills indeed. Eventually my friend's finances improved and she fessed up and bought herself a new copy. (I haven't seen a replacement.) As it happened, she went to the local Chapters. "Oh, that's a great book," the woman behind the cash register said when she paid. Having gone to purchase it with a slight twinge of pride at buying porn, my friend felt deflated. The thrill I experienced buying the same book when I was 15 was gone — not just because we are 15 years older now — but to get the same shiver of transgression you have to be more of a bad girl. A lot more.

Many girls are. Someone like Tisdale, a university-educated writer, can very well be found working in the films Tisdale just watched, bending over at a strip club, donning a nurse uniform for her shift at the dungeon, or having sex with anyone but her partner at a swingers' party. Who hasn't been to a strip club? Your grandmother? Your great-grandmother? A lunchtime martini with the boys at work while a young Russian Svetlana swings her bottom millimeters from your face is so common it's part of an advertising campaign. In a Toronto radio ad, a man calls his girlfriend on his cell phone to tell her he won't be able to see her that evening because he has to work late. As he's talking, a strip club DJ can suddenly be heard announcing the next dancer in the background. "Don't you wish you had text messaging?" the ad asks.

What distinguishes our age from previous ones is that our overall reaction to private behavior is muted. Sure we were in a tizzy over Bill Clinton's affair with Monica Lewinsky, and over Meg Ryan and Russell Crowe's supposed relationship, and even over the exchange of explicit e-mail between a British lawyer and his girlfriend that ended up on computers around the world. But not for long. Liaisons might still be dangerous, but their moral consequences are short-lived.

Still, other people's sexual behavior will be endlessly fascinating to most human beings. Otherwise no one would gossip. We measure ourselves as part of a community. What are the Simpsons doing? Is Homer on Viagra, is Marge swinging in a harness, and if so, where did she buy it? That's why studies about the average number of times that a married couple has sex per week provoke as much of a stir among the right audience as studies on the number of partners a gay man in his early fifties has had in his lifetime provokes in others.

Knowing the stats, however, is not just about prurience. I often find myself asking impolitic questions of people I have just met or encourage my friends to tell me far more than I have the right to know. For a long time I thought this was partly because I have a voyeuristic personality. It comes in handy if you're a journalist. There is more to it than that. If we are to not make a hash of our lives we need to know how others get by. Years of sexual liberation coupled with the pleasure marketplace have made sex a fundamental part of our sense of self.

Every one of the choices we make has similar consequences for our sense of identity, whether or not we made the props, bought them in a store, or have done away with them altogether. We can be polygamous or polyamorous; bisexual, asexual, or transgendered. We can reject gender altogether. At the same time, for straight single women the pressure to be part of a couple is as tremendous as it's ever been, and perhaps more inescapable than it was in the sixties or seventies when you could not fit in and still be part of a community. No wonder the racks of self-help books continue to multiply, the majority of the titles promising emotional protection if only you follow their ten easy rules.

For me the truth is that I've never learnt anything the easy way; not through the warnings of my family or friends, not through reading a book. The other night over dinner, my best friend of almost 15 years said she had always envied what she thought was my ability to become emotionally involved in whatever drama was unfolding in my life. But it's by default, I protested. I can't help but become engrossed, even when it would be better for me to cease and desist.

"No, you feel things," she insisted. I suppose perhaps she is right. But where emotions, particularly women's emotions, are concerned, our society is undecided about which roadmap to follow. Should we put every fragment of our hearts on display or should we deny we have hearts at all?

We live in a confessional culture that at its lowbrow extreme thrives on the lurid talk show and the lurid gossip about famous people no one knows; and on the highbrow end banks on the literary personal memoir, preferably of an abusive, hardship-wracked childhood. A daily flow of emotion permeates our world — no matter how artificial and manufactured the sentiments seem at times — an almost constant glimpse into the lives, hopes and fears of the rest of the strangers who inhabit our neighborhoods, real or virtual. Our own daily worries and anxieties squeeze in between the flotsam of these other lives. I don't believe all this just becomes background entertainment. Other people's dramas, too unimportant to truly engage yet too pervasive to ignore, assault us. Can't cope? The medical establishment will bail you out. Just take this small pink, blue, yellow, white pill, dear, it'll be all right. And shut up. The Western world being the nasty, brutish, competitive, and prosperous place it is, I am in favor of those selective serotonin re-uptake inhibitors pick-me-ups as matter of survival.

What I am not in favor of is the willful denial of the reasons behind why more and more people do turn to anti-depression or anti-anxiety medication, why we are so quick to call our MDs to ask for that prescription. Why do we believe that the world will hurt us in ways that require medical attention? Could our sexual anxieties be partly to blame? Not our Oedipal or Electra complexes, our penis envy or some other Freudian notions, but the daily grind of trying and often failing to get along with at least one other person. All this while living in a world where the detritus of other people's hopes is as close as the woman crying on the streetcar, or the homeless man who at one point was someone's child and someone's lover, asking now for just a quarter. Feeling crazy some of the time is the only way I know I'm still sane.

Every interaction is fraught with parallel possibilities that would have been unthinkable a century ago. For the simplest example turn to the most common romantic scenario that sends women to the proverbial ice cream carton and men to the nearest bar. You're in love with someone, they're not in love with you; or you're in love with someone, they are in love with you, too, and then they're not anymore. It's the oldest story in the book, yes. Nowadays, writing poetry about it is hardly enough.

The relationship is analyzed in hindsight through the prism of gender relations; through any number of pop psychology tomes about loving too much, too fast; professional therapists are called in to stave off the possibility of any such thing happening again; was it you, was it the other person?; does your parents' divorcing (or not divorcing) mean that you were ill-prepared for the demands of a close relationship, or no, too prepared, too cautious? Perhaps the whole model of a two-person couple is defunct, perhaps you (or the other person involved) would have been better off in an open relationship. How wonderful it would be if like Rachel Griffiths in *Me Myself I* or Gwyneth Paltrow in *Sliding Doors* or even Nicholas Cage in *The Family Man*, we could try out different choices, different lives, before making up our minds to commit to the life we're living.

Most of the time, though, I feel like I live in parallel universes anyway. People in my generation have been forcefully encouraged to ask themselves what they want to be, and have had ample opportunity to act on every kind of answer someone could supply to these provocations. We don't just sell sex toys, we sell sexual identities. Whatever your identity problem is, we can solve it if you've got the cash. We can even change bodies to better suit our internal understanding of who we are: men or women. I don't like that sex is for sale, that some of our most intimate selves are being coaxed out in service of the dollar. I would like my sexuality to be isolated from the marketplace. And yet, because sexuality is so very close to the bone, I don't think buying what we want and need in a store or a doctor's office denigrates our humanity. Despite conservative moral opposition and setbacks, the liberal-capitalist premise that individuals must be accorded the fullest liberties and personal protections available under the law to help them reach their zenith of happiness has slowly extended to groups of people who even mere decades ago would have found themselves shunned. Liberalism is as elastic as we demand it to be; in return it demands only that we are able to make peace with our choices.

Would it be too much to call this quest to find ourselves, through trial and error and constant, constant challenge to the accepted norms, noble? From every instance of a man or a woman having sex reassignment surgery to every woman who has ever thrown out her copy of those horrible and imprisoning *Rules*, from huge decisions about one's identity to smaller ones, all these seem to me to be acts of personal courage and self-creation.

"I am wary of sex," says sex writer Lisa Palac in her memoir *The Edge of the Bed*. "Of its transformative powers, its troublesome spells. Flames of passion, hot sex, molten lust, burning desire — it all sounds terribly poetic except for the fact that actually being on fire is terribly painful."[2]

She's right. So it is impossible for me to talk about sex divorced from emotion or separated from love.

In my inability to separate physical pleasure from my feelings, I am also in good company. There is no richer literary tradition than that sown by love. Love and sex invariably change us, sometimes we lose and it is better than never having loved, but the cliché hides the truth that at other times the loss of love is a tragedy from which we emerge as mere shadows of our former selves. I read Carson McCullers's *Ballad of the Sad Café* a few years ago and the vision it presented of the end of love was so terrible that if someone asked me to draw the scene the colors would all be browns and greys and blacks. This is how we first see the woman of the story, years after the man who had lit up her life has vanished. "[On] the second floor there is one window which is not boarded; sometimes in the late afternoon when the heat is at its worst a hand will slowly open the shutter and a face will look down on the town. It is a face like the terrible dim faces known in dreams — sexless and white, with two gray crossed eyes which are turned inward so sharply that they seem to be exchanging with each other one long and secret gaze of grief."[3]

Compared to this wasteland of the heart, sexual practices, no matter how shocking they might seem to some, are just that — a set of behaviors that, should we observe them in an animal on the Discovery channel, would give no pause. Only their adoption by others makes us think and assess our own selves against them. Sex indelibly marks, and our reaction to sexualities marks both the observed and the observers. Without emotion attaching to this, what's there to talk about? X enters Y.

When I was writing this book, I was mostly thinking about women and their lives. After all, it's what I feel most qualified to talk about in the first person. But as feminism has always argued, the issues that bedevil women also affect men. Increasingly, men are questioning and attempting to reshape their identity. Any changes women make in their lives ricochet off and into the lives of men as well. Yet from the perspective of sexuality, particularly heterosexual sexuality, it is women who are doing the majority of the questioning. No longer willing to live in the small safe space between the virgin and the whore, we are trying to become ourselves, whatever that might mean to you or me.

This book, in a way, is a shot at explaining how and what I think about when I think about that quest: parts of my story, parts of the stories of the women in my family, and parts of the stories of my female friends, stories that I have lived, seen, heard (and apologetically hoarded), and tried to disguise from strangers' eyes while still leaving the substance of their tales intact. Statistics can tell one kind of story, to social scientists maybe a more definitive one. Oral histories simply tell of a moment in time, the interpretation up to the listener, or in this case, the reader.

I *have* wondered if growing up during a time when every sexual encounter was thought to have the potential of death, has encouraged me to analyze sex, to take it more seriously than previous generations. An ad from the eighties for Life Styles condoms showed a lovely young woman saying, "I enjoy sex, but I'm not ready to die for it." Imagine having this message, SEX=DEATH, drummed into your head every day as an adolescent. If I am of a generation that is prone to dissembling every encounter, it's because our freedom was for a long time proscribed by our fears. AIDS has become part of our landscape, the yoke under which all our sexual relations live. I understand the desire to "bareback," to have sex without protection. In a roundabout, illogical way, it is a way of thumbing one's nose at danger and death.

I would like one day to hear and tell stories of sex — and of love — to heal our hearts. To tell them because even though they will be marketed in the mall of porn in a shiny box on sale for $19.99, in the telling we come closer to ourselves and closer to hearing others. Not to strip sex of its mystery but to recognize its grace.

CHAPTER **THREE**

BOYS OF SUMMER

"You'd switch off the motor and
turn and reach for me, and I would
Slide into your arms as if I had been born for it . . .
Your front seat had an overpowering male smell, as if the chrome had been
rubbed with jism, a sharp stale
delirious odor like the sour plated
taste of the patina on an old watch, the fragrance of your sex polished till it shone in the night."

— Sharon Olds.[4]

It's a hot summer night in the early 1990s. Along with a small troop of other women I'm walking up Yonge Street, a somewhat seedy thoroughfare dividing Toronto in two. In a couple of days, one of the women in our group will put on a long white bridal dress and walk into a church where she will say her wedding vows as her parents and friends watch and some of them weep. At the moment, however, Sylvia is wearing a very short skirt and a tight white sweater, an outfit which we all more or less match. We've had a few drinks. As we stalk along I imagine we look like a bunch of urban gazelles, on the prowl.

"Hey baby," a guy yells out of a passing car (yet again) and Sylvia yells back "Hey you!" and grins. Unlike some women who, when they're feeling brave, prefer to give such motorists the finger, Sylvia has always smiled back.

"Are we really going to go?" I say.

"Yes!" Sylvia's future sister-in-law exclaims.

When we get to the door of the club, we don't even look up at the sign. We all know where we are, having passed by it so many times and wondered what goes on inside but having never ventured in. During the day, the picture of a shirtless man wearing just a bow tie and a pair of tux pants looks barren and somehow desolate, but at night it lights up and dominates this block of the street. We're at a strip club for women, reached by a set of stairs from the downstairs women's club.

"Hi ladies," the bouncer says and smiles down at us while pocketing the cover charge, $20 each. (The clubs men go to are generally free, since the boys make up the difference through drinks and table dances.) Inside, the lights are dimmed low. Women sit in tight clusters at small tables, their eyes fixed on the stage. A man in a tiny bikini swimsuit is showering on the side of the stage, his body a coil of muscles that have been frequently subjected to the weight machines. He comes out of the shower, towel on his shoulder and begins to elaborately dry himself while dancing. The women holler as he lowers his suit past his hips. To get a peek underneath the suit you have to buy a table dance. A woman runs up and tucks a $5 bill at the top of his trunks. Another slides a bill on the side. The crowd whoops.

Despite the catcalls, the atmosphere is reverent. At the guys' strip club, men chat with each other, casting glances at the girl on stage every once in a while to see if she's their type. Here the women seem hypnotized as if they would be happy to take any or all of the performers home.

We buy Sylvia a table dance and tell the man this is her second last night as a single woman.

"You're getting married, are you?" the man whispers in her ear as he sways his groin near her face. Sylvia blushes and murmurs, "Mmm, you're nice," letting her hands travel over his legs. "You can't do that," he says, smiling, "but since you're getting married . . ."

A chair is at the back of the club, hidden in a shadowy corner. Every ten minutes or so, a new woman sits in the chair and an almost naked man comes and rides over her. The chair is never empty, though the price for 10 minutes can be as much as $50. I look over at one point and see a woman reclining in the chair, her arms dangling at her sides. The man in front of her is pulling his jock strap out of the way to give her a good look. Her expression says she's either drunk or in heaven, her face speaks of abandon.

Women looking at men. We so rarely talk about how it makes us feel. Sure, like men, women have become adept at joking about men's asses, their biceps, their shoulders, their pecs, their cocks. We talk and laugh, embarrassed. We never say we find men awe-inspiring.

The first time I felt desire I was quite young; a lot of people would say that what I felt was a childhood kind of lust, and they are probably right. As a kid I watched the boys playing, the muscles in their legs and arms and shoulders tensing and developed big, huge crushes.

In the summer of 1988 desire swept me off my proverbial feet; it happened after exchanging nothing more than a few looks with one of my neighborhood's high-school truants.

I spent much of that summer walking or biking around the Beach, a pretty neighborhood by Lake Ontario in the east end of Toronto. My arms are tanned, the muscles in my calves taut from the constant exercise. As the summer wears on, I start noticing a boy. He has brown hair, brown eyes, and a goatee (it *was* 1988) and we start making eye contact as I bike by. One day I stop right on the bench where he sits with his friends. He's wearing a t-shirt and baggy jeans and combat boots. I stare at him, we exchange names. I notice that he has sunken cheeks, which I immediately like. Then I notice that in spite of the fact that he's not a very big guy, he has muscles in his upper arms.

He asks me to go to a movie with him later on that night. We go to see a British comedy about a working-class guy falling in love with a woman while trying to hold on to his construction job. Afterwards, he asks if I want to go for a bike ride down to the beach. It's the stereotypical beautiful night — the air is cool and we sit up talking about whatever it is that teenagers talk about, the rhythm of the water, the night sky, the stars. After four or five hours of this, he turns to me and kisses me. And it's over. I'd been kissed before but never like that.

Since then, there have been points in my life where I have desired someone very much — and then the fear of being swallowed whole takes over. Will I always be able to do nothing but think of the man I want, be quite happy doing nothing more world-changing than tracing the outline of his collarbone and the line of his eyebrows over and over and over again? The fear comes from being scared of giving in to this, of losing control, of losing myself in another. And eventually of losing them. Of course, by the time I feel this way with someone, I'm already lost.

Women get as attached to bodies as men. When those bodies are gone we can spend months lying in bed at night, unable to sleep, able only to conjure up the beloved in our minds and wondering if we will ever feel better or if the torment is permanent. In some ways it amazes me that we are all capable of falling that far in lust with another body, of needing another body so much, over and over again, despite losing those bodies.

When we do lose them, the whole world seems to turn rancid. I'm not the first to point out that a day of sunshine when your heart is broken seems like an insult. We want to see ourselves reflected in the world and if we're broken what right do the birds have to sing?

One summer I was going through a particularly difficult break-up. The weather was hot and sticky and humid, the sun blazing every day, the kind of weather perfect for swimming outside, something I would normally love to do. Not that summer. What I remember is that everything I came into contact with, and even my body, seemed putrid. My skin broke out in hives. One day by mistake I left the screen door to the deck open during the day when I went to work. I closed it when I got home, but when I went to bed that night I passed by the door and saw hundreds of huge black flies, seemingly attracted by my black mood. A summer of feeding on rotting food in the heat had made them juicy and repulsive. Another day I baked a roast chicken. I forgot the carcass inside the stove for only a day and a half. The stench when I pulled out the pan was terrible. Maggots were crawling over the bones. This is what desire can turn into.

One night that summer I rent a movie with my best friend and we sit in the basement, where it's cool. In it, Tommy Lee Jones is husband to an especially high-strung Jessica Lange; they live on a variety of army bases and Lange is always the sexiest, liveliest presence around. In one scene, as a dance hall full of army staff and their spouses look on, Lange gets drunk, then proceeds to come on to every soldier there. Some wife he's got there, says the look on the face of every one who then watches Jones dance with his wife and eventually throw her over his shoulder and carry her home. Break-ups have always robbed me of this sense of exuberant lust.

I've recognized the feeling in few places. As a teenager, I somehow stumbled onto a copy of Jean Genet's *Miracle of the Rose*, the gay French writer's fictionalized memoir of his many years in a boys' reformatory, and later, in jail. I read it when I was about 14. His ecstatic writing about men's bodies made my teenage hormones jump. Every page in the book drips with sex and desire: poetic, lyrical, idealized images of men as gods who hold Genet's happiness in their hands. "I ascribe everything to his good looks, to his blond curls, his cruel eyes, his teeth, his bare throat, his exposed chest, to the most precious part of him,"[5] he wrote, and an enthusiastic teenage girl was only too happy to finally find someone who was as kookily mystical about men as she was.

In mainstream culture, women's desires are more often than not derided. In one episode of the TV series *Ally McBeal*, one of the series by which women's lives have been measured for a couple of years, the women at the law firm enroll in an art class. To their delighted surprise, the male model assigned to the class has a huge penis. Ally sleeps with him. Just to score a large-membered male specimen. In the end, she realizes she can't just date him for his body (maybe only because the series is written by a man.) In another episode, Ally has wanton sex with a man she meets at a car wash. Right there, on the spot. This in the same season that she kisses a woman. The message seemed not to be so much that Ally is at long last emerging from her illusory romantic bubble into a full-blown, full-blooded sexual woman, but that she is out of control, unaware even of what she wants.

While writing this chapter, I came upon a book at the local literary chain. It had a blue, textbook-like cover with simply its title and the authors' names. *Sexually Aggressive Women*, it screamed out, and though the price was also textbook ($79.95) and it was clearly aimed at professional therapists, I couldn't help but wonder why the publishing house hadn't thought to make the most of its title and produce a flashy, glossy edition with a picture of Glenn Close, wife-murdering knife in hand. The authors could have made a killing, not to mention gotten themselves on just about every talk show in America.[6]

After all, the contents were incendiary enough. The book's aim was nothing less than to implode the theory of women as sexual victims of men's aggression. Far from always being sugar and spice and everything nice, women could be relied on as much as men to make unwanted sexual advances, sometimes escalating those advances from verbal pressure to physical threats. Almost 30 per cent of college men surveyed in one section had experienced such an incident from a female. The survey had not investigated what percentage of women perpetuate such attacks (or how many of them would admit to doing so).

Aside from the statistical information, the book was also rich in anecdotal evidence from men. Most of our boys had drunk too much (in the book's wisdom the women had gotten them drunk), or had had a late night at a girl's house when the incident occurred. The come-ons ranged from spoken inducements to sex, to women grabbing the men's penises, to women giving the men blowjobs before being stopped. (This latter event was reported often enough to beg the question as to what the guy was doing when the woman unbuttoned his pants.) Enough such stories were shared that they formed a compendium of female misbehavior, of what women will do when drunk enough or horny enough, or simply pre-menstrual enough to risk making idiots of themselves.

If this all sounds as if I'm making light of the men's plight, it's because the overwhelming majority of men did not themselves think the event merited more than a footnote in their personal histories. The degree to which men felt the incident was traumatic was directly proportional to how attractive they judged the women to be. Even if they were not interested, when the woman was attractive, the incident invariably rated a 1 or 2 on a seven-point scale of trauma.

The last chapter in the book was particularly revealing. A short manual on how to treat sexually aggressive women, it suggested therapy as well as greater public awareness of women's power to do sexual harm to men. I would not dispute that men can be made uncomfortable by a woman's advances and that because in a lot of the book's anecdotal cases the parties involved were already acquaintances, there is no easy way to say no to someone you will see again. And that women's threats of violence can be as frightening as a man's. Yet, as the men themselves admitted, they were never scared: they knew their physical strength protected them. Their discomfort was emotional, more on the level of what a woman feels when she does not want to have intercourse with a man for a variety of emotional reasons. She doesn't like him that much, the sex is a precursor to a relationship she doesn't want, or she wants a relationship and the sex is clearly not a precursor to that.

Ironically, the men had news for all the women who believe men would love to have sex without the complications of a relationship. Seems that men aren't all that different from women (who, as we all know, look at an opened box of condoms as just the pause before the inevitable baby carriage). A remarkable number of the men in the book did not want to have sex with the women who propositioned them because they felt they were just being used as one-night stands.

The book's aim must be something other than warning away wily sexual predators. Certainly, I had been looking for something else when I spotted it on the shelf. I began reading it standing up, but soon enough I was sitting in the aisle, biting the polish off my nails, engrossed, having forgotten what it was that had brought me inside the bookstore in the first place. Here was a book that confirmed my worst, neurotic suspicions about a couple of incidents in my own personal life. Never have I grabbed a man's cock or given a blowjob when such action would have been clearly unwelcome. (Reading about these women who had, whose brazenness was sure to provide some man with some very fond memories in his old age, I felt a rush of envy and admiration.)

I have, however, been scorned — and I'd like to think I'm not alone in this — have pleaded, cried, and caused minor dramatic scenes. Depending on my mood, I think back on these incidents and congratulate myself for either having a flare for drama or self-flagellate for having a flare for drama. To those thoughts I now added a fearful one: I was also a statistic, on the bunny boiler scale I merited at least a small mention.

More importantly, the book left me with fear not only about the couple of times I'd maybe strayed on to the wrong side of the sexual aggression equation, but also with fear about the times when my come-ons had been welcome. Maybe that was wrong too, maybe it's wrong to sidle up to a boy and slide your hands under his t-shirt then wrestle him to the bed; maybe it's even wrong to kiss the boy first. Maybe I should have always waited. Maybe I should have always been good.

In one half-hour of skimming, the authors had turned me into a woman terrified of my own desires and certainly terrified to act on them. If I'd had a date that night, I probably would have dressed head-to-toe in loose black sackcloth and forgotten to wash my hair, all just to make sure that I wasn't giving off any unwanted sexual vibes. For sure, I overreacted. In my defense, my scenes were too complicated to be captured in a statistic; my victories, as it were, praised long after their recipients and I had parted ways. More importantly, each time I'd never doubted for a moment that I was alive in ways that my day-to-day life did not often afford, in ways that stripped me of my intellectual bent, of my cerebralism, of my logic, and turned me into a simple mass of hormones and overwhelming emotion. It can make you want to kill yourself but it also makes you want to live a little while longer, if only to feel that way again. All this for lust.

A friend of mine once told me how she used to pick her boyfriends. On the first date, or more likely, after a particularly drunk night spent in the company of lots of other people, she and a guy would head home. There were no preliminaries for her. If they hit it off in the sack, she would consider him as boyfriend material. She never had any doubts that he himself was interested in repeating the experience. If you read the books warning women that such behavior leads to a broken heart, you would never believe that my friend is now married to someone who was road-tested in exactly this way. The book's point, however, was precisely to strangle this fearless female confidence in getting what we want instead of worrying about who wants or doesn't want us.

As women, one of our dirty secrets is how good we are at policing each other's desires, at sometimes taking each other's weakest points and insecurities and turning them against each other.

In the early nineties I worked for a time as an editor at the student newspaper. In theory, this is supposed to be a part-time job. In reality it's full-time which in turn means I am there all the time.

My boyfriend also works at the paper and at the end of each day we make our way home where we have sex until we pass out exhausted. He's relatively new (six months or so) at this point; we're relatively young (22); and we have few other responsibilities outside of going to the paper and maybe showing up to our few classes during the day. The latter falls by the wayside of course. We are also perennially late — every morning around 10:30 the phone rings and the paper's editor asks when we think we're going to show up.

I'm wearing a blue cotton turtleneck sweater because at some point in our enthusiasm the night before I have ended up with a hickey as purple and obvious as any of the ones I'd seen on classmates in junior highschool. During those days, the hicky-ed and the non-hickey-ed lived in two separate camps: the first indicated that it was quite likely you were having sex, the latter meant either you were not or no one knew about it. One day, one of the handsomest boys in our grade nine typing class came in wearing a white shirt, black jeans, and a hickey. The boys slapped him on the back, the girls cast envious glances at his hickey or giggled. Did they want to be the one who'd given it to him or did they wonder what he'd given his girlfriend in return? His girlfriend, on the other hand, was already developing a reputation. A girl who'd grown size C breasts at the age of 13, her hips and thighs were always encased in jeans that she squeezed into when they were wet (as she told everyone) and her reddish, shoulder-length mane was always hair-sprayed so that the fringes of her bangs touched her eyelashes. She was va-va-vavoom and she was a slut. She, too, often had a hickey. It had taken me just about a decade, but finally I was, much as I had wanted, just like her.

"What is that?" asked a woman who was sitting at a computer next to mine.

"Oh, shit," I said and raised the collar of my turtleneck a little higher. Inside I was proud.

By the end of the afternoon, the news that I had a hickey had spread throughout the building. To this day I have not been able to figure out the reasons for the reaction I got: a mixture of raised eyebrows, wide avoidance maneuvers, and from one woman, a derisive snort. The best hypothesis I could come up with was that the hickey, combined with my constant tardiness, was evidence that I had allowed my desires to get the upper hand over my intellectual interests, a slap in the face of the strongly feminist environment in which I worked (and was, otherwise, quite happy to be a part of). What had I been doing while some of the other women in the office were already working? Lying in bed.

This was the early 1990s, before feminism incorporated sex-positive feminism, before liking, wanting, lusting after sex, was accepted, and indeed encouraged, as a sign of feminist commitment. I didn't like this. I wanted someone to come up and hi-five me as I adjusted my bra strap: "Hey good going Chiose! Got some last night, huh?"

In so many ways, though, the reaction of the women I was working with made more sense and still makes more sense to me than the call to sexual arms issued by the sex-positivists. Sexual desire is dangerous, it does have the power to keep a girl in bed when she really should be out there working on her career, engaging with the world. Sexual desire does not allow the world in; instead it shuts it out, making "the two of us here" the only world. Lust messes with one's mind, making it wander to the body of our lover when we should be thinking about a paper or a project due the day before.

There was something very right about the frenzy surrounding Bill Clinton's affair with Monica Lewinsky: for once, popular culture, which every day of the year feeds us images of desire with our morning paper, on highway billboards, and on the pages of every magazine and TV screen, was stopped in its tracks by the power of one woman's desire for one man. She saw, she liked, she showed thong, she ended up on her knees. The outcome for everyone was not ideal, but for Lewinsky in particular, it turned her lusty crush into humiliation.

A woman in the throes of romantic passion was, and is, seen as unmanageable. In the 19th century, one of the most frequent treatments for female hysteria was for the doctor to masturbate the patient to orgasm. The vibrator and the dildo were born to help doctors calm insane nymphomaniacs. Make her come and you tame her.[7] Women's desires are still medicalized away. "When people tell me I'm too intense," writes Wendy Shalit in her troubling *Return to Modesty*, "they are saying, you care? How embarrassing for you. You're emotionally vulnerable? . . . If it's hard for you to be indifferent about sex, just try harder. Take Prozac."[8] I agree with her that women's behavior is pathologized simply because it's inconvenient to have a weeping woman around, especially in the current go, go, go economic system where excessive emotion interferes with productivity. But Shalit's solution dumps that bigger issue right back on women's lap. Instead of encouraging both men and women to demand respect in and out of bed, she tells women to go back to repressing their sexuality. Who needs Prozac if you never take enough risks to be hurt in the first place?

I do understand why Shalit reached this conclusion. If you can't afford to lose much, if in your daily life you don't have much power, you're not going to allow desire to sweep you off your feet. Only the powerful can allow themselves to give free reign to their lusts and few women feel themselves on top of the world like that.

But not feeling desire is just as dangerous. Women become neurotic, second-guessing ourselves at every turn. More importantly, we allow the world to second-guess us as well. No one is as easy to control as a woman who no longer wants anything, who has ceased wanting before anyone has told her she can't have. When we don't look at men as objects of our physical desire we are saying no to ourselves. The repression slowly enters all aspects of our life.

But forget modern manuals of taming the wild woman within for the benefit of men; all that good little girls have to read to stay good is *Anna Karenina.* A fearful tale if there ever was one, it ends with Anna madly throwing herself under the wheels of a train after she imagines Count Vronsky has tired of her.

When I first read *Anna Karenina* I was an impressionable teenager. I wasn't reading for the nuances of Russian society, for the place of women in that society. I read it as a warning about the evil men do — Vronsky after all loves Anna when she is unattainable, when she is still torn between him and her family, when their moments are clandestine, stolen. As soon as he becomes her main man, and her sole source of support, he becomes increasingly resentful of her.

But at the same time, Anna was enormously appealing, the most romantically fearless of heroines. She is convinced of the strength of Vronsky's love, she is passionate, she has no sense. Her husband and child fade when confronted with the power of her desire. And if in the end she dies, in the time she spends with Vronsky she seems to live with as much passion as any young woman alive 150 years later.

And this perhaps is ultimately why women have not allowed themselves to look at men the way they look at us. Much as we want to be fearless romantic heroines, we are also scared of ourselves and especially of what we see other women reduced to when in love. Desire undoes women the same way it undoes men. Men move on, though, to the next piece of jailbait, or to the next woman who will break their hearts. (Or at least they do a better job of pretending to move on. In reality, women are the real survivors.) Desire undoes women publicly. It may not throw us under moving trains but it makes us make spectacles of ourselves. Nothing seems to bother and frighten women more than the sight of a sister who's come undone because of her love for a man. It's a state we never wish upon ourselves.

"Yes, I am a woman," wrote Emma Goldman to her lover Ben Reitman, "indeed too much of it. . . . I was caught in the torrent of an elemental passion I had never dreamed any man could rouse in me. I responded shamelessly to its primitive call. . . . That's my tragedy."[9] Or as Simone de Beauvoir put it, woman "succeeds in losing all her attractiveness" when she resorts to "tears, demands, and scenes."[10] Less elegant, but no less true, how many times have I listened to girlfriends describing how they ripped up pictures of their men, slammed phones and threw lamps? How many times have I made demands and ended up in tears?

Often, when I'm out in a restaurant, I'll survey the couples at other tables. One day I saw two people who were clearly on their second, or perhaps third, date. He was explaining how optics work. They were staring in each other's eyes. She was leaning closer and closer toward him. Suddenly, she leaned back and didn't lean forward again. I think it's because she was worried he might see how deeply he was affecting her.

But in not letting ourselves look at men for as long as we want, or in choosing to not even look in the first place, we cut ourselves off. Desire is big and scary and frightening. Even in a loving relationship, it's the scariest thing a person can feel. As a friend of mine says, desire is the ultimate humbling experience. You can be awed by a work of art and walk away after a few minutes of gazing at it. To be awed by a person and their beauty, by a person who can hurt you at any point, whether they mean to or not, leaves one vulnerable and exposed in a way that only children are.

When "the erotic and the tender are mixed in a woman, they form a powerful bond, almost a fixation,"[11] said Anais Nin, and it is this sentiment which distinguishes a woman really looking at a man and this which scares us. When we look at a man we know and love, we want to see. Some porn images focus on the face of the woman at the moment of (pretend) orgasm. To me, this is much more intimate and so much more erotically powerful than countless close-up shots of genitalia and hard-to-achieve gymnastic positions. I wish I'd see a single movie which focuses on a man's face at that exact moment.

I have no idea if women's erotic gaze is socialized to include tenderness or if it is a gender characteristic, part and parcel of being able to express (or being taught) compassion. Quite likely it's the former. As the literary critic Peter Lehman says, women are taught from childhood to "see with their hearts, not eyes."[12] What matters is that at its most potent, most able to inspire deep longing, looking means looking with love. Think of Meryl Streep waking in the middle of the night and sitting up, her hand hovering over the naked torso of the sleeping Clint Eastwood in *The Bridges of Madison County*. He doesn't wake up and the next morning, when she throws a fit and asks him what, if anything, their short-lived affair means to him, he is at first blown back by her outburst. Women "cannot even let men know the scope of their desire because the men could not handle it," Lehman says and how right he is.[13]

Eastwood provokes this even though he is a man who appears to be in his sixties, his face deeply lined, his chest not meriting any lingering close-ups in the movie. He is still very handsome, but no longer the picture of male perfection, a copy of the smooth lines of a Greek statue. Whatever problems the movie has — sentimentalism, Streep's stark choices — it captures perfectly the tenor of impassioned female desire.

What else is the movie but a version of *Beauty and the Beast*, another fairy tale about a woman's love changing an inhuman creature into the most beautiful thing in the world? In Eastwood's case, changing him from a lone wanderer into a domesticated man willing to share his travels with another. If there is beauty in the eye of the beholder it can make its object rise to its gaze. Think of Roxanne, blinded by her lover's beauty, not even willing to look poor Cyrano's way twice. How much happier her life could have been had she fallen in love with Cyrano from the first.

Few women are cool observers of a man's body. The British writer Sarah Kent says that for her a photo of a man's genitals is not just a voyeuristic object — the way a similar photo of a woman presumably could be — but the preservation of a memory of intimacy and pleasure.

In 1997, the Croatian writer Slavenka Drakulic published *The Taste of a Man*. The book's heroine falls in love with a man who is teaching in New York temporarily, his wife and children back home in Brazil. The narrator's desire eventually leads her to kill her lover and eat him, turning what could have been just a fading memory of him into her flesh. Threatened with his loss, she can do nothing but refuse to let him go: what starts out as an insane escape from the certainty that there is an end to their mutual desire appears almost logical. If he leaves, she goes mad. This way, she goes mad but he stays.

For some reason, I have sometimes brought up the book when talking to people I've been interested in. The way other people sometime give warnings about their shortcomings, the way other people say "I have trouble saying I love you," I want to say I will, I may, it may occur, that at times I will love you too much and it will scare me and because the fear of losing you will be so big it will make me think of this book. I don't, of course, say all this. I just explain the book. From the look on the faces of the men with whom I've had a snippet of this conversation I have a pretty good idea of whether they'd be up for me.

I've always had a love-hate relationship with the phenomenon of the rock star. I hate the bravado and the posturing that all too often hides a distinct lack of talent. Yet rock music is the only place where a raw response to raw sexuality is encouraged. We have lost most of the other traditions and rituals binding us to our ancestors; but we are rarely more primitive than when going to a rock show where the musicians are not just artists (or not even artists) but sacrificial sexual lambs. With a twist of their hip some musicians can inspire screams that others couldn't match if they dropped their trousers. I remember reviewing a concert by David Bowie. Already in his early 50s, Bowie was playing a smallish club in Toronto and because posters of his face used to adorn my high-school locker, I squeezed into the front row. He was wearing no shoes, a loose pair of black sultan pants and a purple shirt. His toenails were painted black and though he didn't gyrate the way Mick Jagger does when he sets hearts aflutter, a simple swing of his hips and a kick in the air was enough to send me into paroxysms of delight. If I were to ever interview him, I could never tell him this. Of course. We would talk about his art and his wife, the model Iman. On stage, though, rock stars are our fantasies made real.

Every woman has her rock star type. As we grow older, our real-life preferences differ more and more from the false idols we worship. I wouldn't want to go out with Jim Morrison, but at one time, I was searching for his double. I wouldn't want to go out with Prince, but his sensuality is irresistible. For a while, the unbridled fury of Axl Rose even made up for his misogyny and homophobia. These latter-day icons differ from those of the fifties or sixties. Elvis or the Beatles dressed up their sexiness in an armor of romance. Elvis could wiggle his pelvis one minute, but before the girls got too scared he whispered words of tenderness. John and Paul had more going on with each other for much of the time than with the audience. Morrison may have suggested that he was interested in one thing and one thing only but he was a tortured soul on the side, happier exorcising his demons — *"Mother, I'm going to fuck you"* — than keeping anyone's fires lit.

Rose, on the other hand, has never been anything but bad news. I remember videos of his concert performances, Axl parading in a pair of short and tight boxer shorts, asking all the girls to be his sweet child.

"Do you think that's his real penis?" a male friend asked one day when Axl graced the TV screen. But it wasn't Axl's apparently large size that interested me as much as the whole package. He was object and subject at the same time, offering himself the same way Elvis did, but with a sneer on his face that promised only ill would come of anyone who took up his offer. Had the invitation been personally extended, had I known that no one would know, and nothing too terrible would happen, I doubt I would have ever said no to an hour with the guy.

Step outside the concert hall and women control themselves. In daily life, we lack the language, either verbal or visual, that men have developed about women. Male photographers have long documented the intimate details of women's bodies and lives. Women have been slower to capture equivalent images on film. Elinor Carucci has photographed her husband and herself at home, she bent over the toilet with cramps or with hair bleach on her belly; he sleeping or eating. Sally Mann's snapshots document her life with her husband, from mundane moments to lovemaking. But how many people are looking for either of their works? Not accustomed to seeing language that reflects our own feelings about desire, we remain silent. (And encouraged to stay that way. After Mann casually showed some of the work featuring her husband as part of a lecture at the Virginia Museum of Fine Arts, the museum received a letter complaining about the explicit nature of some of the photos.)

A few women I've spoken to have confessed that images of gay porn turn them on more than beefcake in *Playgirl.* In gay movies, not all of the men are dominant all of the time and the camera possesses them in the way the lens usually owns a woman. Take Bruce La Bruce's independent *Hustler White.* In it, the trim, blond director plays a man hopelessly infatuated with a young hustler. Dressed in jeans and a white t-shirt, the hustler relishes the camera panning over his body, taking in his torso, his arm, his shoulders, all in slow motion. The sequence is extraordinarily lingering and dreamy. When I first saw it, the first thing I thought was 'how come women don't shoot men like that?'

For thousands of years, female models have inspired male artists, but few male models have served the same function for women. Looking at naked men, even in the interests of education, was just not done. In 1893, the Pennsylvania Academy of Fine Arts introduced male models in classes attended by both men and women. Shortly afterward, James L. Claghorn received a letter from one of the female students' mothers. "Does it pay for a young lady of a refined godly household to be urged as the only way of obtaining a knowledge of true Art, to enter a class where every feeling of maidenly delicacy is violated," she asked the liberal president.[14] Change comes slowly.

If it's taken thousands of years for men to objectify women, surely it takes some time for women to learn to objectify men. I'm still figuring it out. For years and years now, when I walk down the street my eye is much more often drawn to women than to men. To what they're wearing, to their lipstick, to their hair color. I can appreciate an attractive woman much easier than an attractive man, yet I've never been in a relationship with one. Everyone is taught to look at women. As film critic Laura Mulvey said back in 1977, the male gaze defines women whether we are the ones looking or the ones being looked at. Women are each other's harshest critics and most ardent admirers because we look the same way men do. And then we look some more. We know what it's like to be assessed. If we are more forgiving of male physical flaws perhaps it's not just because we place more value on men's emotional qualities than their physical beauty, but also because we don't look at them all that closely.

And men prefer it that way. The male psyche is still dealing with the explosion of male nudity that started in the 1980s. Boys are flocking to gyms not just to be healthy, but because the bellies women say we don't care about (and most of the time we mean it) are nowhere to be seen on the flat abs of the men on the big and small screens. When John Doe gazes upon a Calvin Klein underwear ad, his ego suffers a little bit. Gaze upon it every day and pretty soon he might feel a creeping loss of his own humanity, gut and flab and all. "Everybody wants to have sex with you," bodybuilder Kerwin Scott told writer Susan Faludi, "but only because they want to see what you look like in bed."[15] If even bodybuilders feel this way, imagine what the rest of the gang is going through.

Until recently, few straight men have been willing to put themselves in that position. The classic movie stars on whom our notions of masculinity are based were humiliated when they were sold on their looks. "I took off my jacket and shirt, bared my chest and flexed my muscles . . . I was probably the only man in Hollywood who's had to strip to get a part," said Kirk Douglas of his audition for 1949's *Champion.* "The women ogled me, as if they were looking right through my clothes."[16]

Even now, the men we revere who take off their clothes bolster their virility by holding a gun when they're shirtless. Think Stallone or Schwarzenegger. In the real world, brawn doesn't have much value. All a computer programmer needs to bring home the bacon is his calculator-like mind. Meanwhile the gals are looking at naked pictures of hunky men on the Net. Is it really a coincidence that just as women are ogling men more, men are coming up with ever more explicit images of women in mainstream magazines like *Maxim*? Now that we have male and female eye candy, you have to strip down a woman more often and in more venues to assert your masculine dominance.

Like this, slowly, in missteps and mistakes, we are developing our own language of desire. I remember a few years ago when *The Piano* came out. I was working for a newspaper at the time and at the desk next to mine, a woman had pinned up a publicity shot of Harvey Keitel. In his cabin in the woods, Keitel was naked from the waist up and bent over Holly Hunter sitting at the piano. My co-worker and her friend would swoon over his body all day long. By all conventional standards, the actor's body is not beautiful. Hunched shoulders and bad posture, a large belly and aged skin — no Ralph Lauren ad would dare feature him in anything but baggy pants and a wool turtleneck sweater.

Through Jane Campion's eyes, her camera lingering over his naked body, a symbol of all the desire that awakens Holly Hunter, Keitel became beautiful, all the more beautiful for his flaws. If the fresh-faced Kate Hudson is every teenage boy's current dream girl, Keitel was the thinking woman's sex object.

I was 25 when I heard these women salivating over him. I would listen to them talk and marvel at the openness with which they did so. It was quite simply wonderful, as if all of a sudden women had not just been allowed into the locker room, but taken it over.

Every once in a while I'll see a man I find really striking walking down the street. The look I give him most closely resembles a look I've only seen one male friend of mine give women. It's pure lust and assessment and fantasy all rolled into one. The feeling when I see these men is visceral, it's wanting to take a camera and photograph that man's entire body. I've only ogled like this when I know there is no chance of having to talk to the guy — like if I'm speeding by on a bike really fast. Certainly it's easier to gaze at a lover, but even then I rarely seem to — a feeling of goofiness holds me back as if I can see myself in some female-version of *Miami Vice* and sorely don't want to find myself in any such locale. Still, women can be just as visually stimulated as men; when one man combines sexiness, intellectual rapport, and emotional connection, well, then he's got a pressure cooker of a woman to deal with.

Reed-thin male bodies or muscled ones look back at you from the pages of any magazine. Alone, or coupled with women, these bodies rarely say anything to me and even more rarely fill me with hunger. The male ideal may be Adonis, but I'd like to see more pictures in the mainstream media taken by people who have a stake in the subject. Maybe then we'd know what desire looks like.

There was one time I did take photos of a boyfriend. What I remember most is the exhilarating power of it, the feeling that comes with giving orders from behind the camera. I was 19 or 20 at the time. The desire I had for him was absolutely pure. We would lie in bed for hours just sleeping, or napping, without worrying about what would happen the next day. In the whole time I was with him I know we had many fights and many times, especially during our first year together, they ended with me in tears. Things, in other words, were not perfect. But what I remember best is that I never repressed my desire for him. Only after more relationships, when love became tinged with fear and anxiety and regret of other loves I had lost, did I begin to wonder about women and men. About why we want them so freely when we're young and slow ourselves as we get older. What is it that forces our eyes underground?

CHAPTER **FOUR**

HEY, BABY

"The filly Tulsy Tsan was withdrawn from a race in New Zealand last week when authorities discovered that her name read 'nasty slut' backwards. The horse has now been renamed 'Ben Again' and returned to the track later in the week."[17]

It was after a grade seven field trip that I first learnt the meaning of the word slut. That's when the school's resident "woman" almost gave the school's resident "loser" a blowjob while her friends watched.

All the grade sevens and grade eights were shepherded onto school buses destined for the Don Valley Ravine, a Toronto park that stretches for kilometers: the city's suburban Central Park. Paved roads wind their way through the park while hikers make paths in the woods. The landscape of trees and scraggly bushes is broken up by meadows, clearings appearing out of nowhere and depending on the day and the weather, sometimes deserted, sometimes swarming with families on a picnic.

When I was a teenager I lived in a high-rise apartment across from the ravine and the more time I spent in the park the more I thought it could be dubbed Sex Central. A couple of times I ran into flashers. They would open their trench coats and I would bike faster, catching a glimpse of what they had to show me only out of the corner of my eye.

At night, young couples making out in their cars, or in the summer, by the banks of the Don River, vastly outnumbered the flashers.

The purpose of the trip was to study the Ravine's ecosystem and the pollution in the river. We were on our own for lunch, free to wander off to one of the scattered food outlets in the park if we could make it back in time, or to eat whatever we'd brought from home. As lunch was coming to an end a rumor seeped up from the clusters of kids sitting on picnic benches.

"Kristin blew Peter, Kristin blew Peter." Boys passed by the table where Peter was sitting, taunting him. I wasn't sure what they said because at the time I don't think I understood what had happened. What I recall most is the animated hush that fell over the end of that lunch hour as if something unspeakable had risen from among us and naming it could shut down the school. Questions about what we were going to do in the afternoon, any questions to the teachers at all really, were answered in few words and by grim faces. Conversations between the kids had dropped to a whisper.

Kristin sat at a table next to one of her boyfriends not saying anything. Most likely, she was smoking one of her ever-present cigarettes. Unlike many of the girls in grade seven who hadn't even kissed yet, she had more than a few boys around her at all times. Rumor had it she was sleeping with all of them.

The version of the story which eventually reached me was this: Kristin had arranged with her friends to lure Peter into taking a walk away from everyone else. As we all knew, he nursed a huge crush on her. He lurked by her locker after school, tried to talk to her in every class they shared, and occasionally got mad and sulky when she simply pretended he was not there. When she acknowledged his existence, she did it by laughing and walking away, without the proverbial backward glance. He was her flipside. As unpopular as she was popular, as out-of-place as she fit right into the cliquish world of junior high. Like the men she did pay attention to, Peter wore a leather motorcycle jacket, t-shirts with three-quarter length sleeves and with the names of heavy metal bands on the front and tour dates on the back. Awkward and always enthusiastic about everything, especially these bands, he lacked the unapproachable, silent charm that made Kristin's boys the objects of all the girls' fantasies.

At a certain point in the walk, Kristin got Peter to stop and drop his pants and underwear on the pretext that she was going to give him a blowjob. As soon as he did so, Kristin's friends, boys and girls, jumped out of the bushes around them. Terrified and ashamed, Peter scampered into his clothes and ran like mad back to the group having lunch.

The prank had been on him but within a few months of the incident, the nasty things which had been whispered about Kristin before were now said outright. By grade ten, her stock had plummeted altogether: she was no longer even talked about.

Right after the "incident," however, I documented the whole thing in the diary our English teacher had instructed all her students to keep. The diary was a private thing. Once a month, we went up to her desk and opened it to where she had last marked it. She quickly flipped through the pages making sure they were not all filled with "all work and no play makes Jack a dull boy" and put a red check mark at the end of our last entry. She didn't read what we wrote. This diary I thought was safe at the back of a closet in my bedroom. Not safe enough for my parents' curious eyes.

One late evening, I was summoned for a conference on the contents of the diary, the entry on Kristin and Peter's escapade entered as evidence. "Why was I writing about this? None of it could have possibly happened, why was I making it up?" It happened, I don't know, it was crazy, everyone talked about it at school, I spluttered in between protests at their having opened and read the book that was marked VERY PRIVATE DO NOT READ!!! Eventually one of them threw the gauntlet down: "Do you want to end up like her? A slut! Do you know what men think of sluts?!"

Oh yes please! I said in my head but I also knew to think that was wrong. As a very inexperienced 14-year-old, all I really knew was that men didn't want to date (much less marry!) a slut, a girl they didn't have to coax into sex. Worse, that once they did have sex, they would move on to the next woman, abandoning the slut and condemning her to wonder why she always ended up alone. I'm not sure how I had picked all this up. Much as I envied Kristin I also feared her life. The truth is that for a long time, before the advent of women affectionately calling themselves "ethical sluts," "bitches," and "ho's," no one wanted to be called a slut. Yet a lot of girls have felt the sting.

When the American Association of University Women conducted a poll on sexual harassment in schools in 1992, it found that 42 per cent of girls had had sexual rumors spread about them.[18] Even now, when I hear the word it provokes at least instant suspicion of the person who uttered it to describe a woman. Quite simply, I find it repellent.

Because of "slut," women followed the sexual script: stick to a complicated set of rules about your sexual behavior, or transgress them and be ostracized. Whether it's as adolescents or adults, women have felt what Naomi Wolf memorably called "the shadow slut" walking beside them. Is my skirt too short, too tight, not short enough, not tight enough, should I have slept with that person on the first date? In 1919, a columnist for *A Woman's Home Companion* magazine told the story of a girl who fell in love with a man. The girl allowed him "liberties" though they were not engaged. At the time, that meant kissing. Soon after he left her.[19]

The line from the Bible, to 1919, and from 1919 to 2001 is unbroken in its insistence on female chastity. Should the wedding night reveal that the woman has already been deflowered, at least we no longer follow the Good Book's advice: "[If] the tokens of virginity be not found for the damsel: Then they shall bring out the damsel to the door of her father's house, and the men of her city shall stone her with stones that she die."[20]

Fallen women are a threat, outside the control of father, state, and society. Now we throw prostitutes in jail; in medieval times, some city governments ran brothels. Florentine prostitutes of the 15th century had no way back to grace save for entering monasteries for their kind. The first such place was established in 1227 and was called The

Order of Saint Mary Magdalene. Chastity was the highest female virtue, but because women in Florence did not always comply, establishing brothels was the scarlet letter that separated the virtuous from the indulgent.

In Victorian London, it was poor women who were sluts. To the chagrin of religious authorities, the working classes were spending their pennies in public houses, outside the walls of the home. Commoners' pastimes were described in disgusted tones by those who appointed themselves chroniclers of the ways of the fallen: "One missionary knocked [at a tavern door] in the middle of the day. . . . He saw two young men and two young women dancing together, all in an entire state of nudity, a fiddler playing in another part of the room, while they danced," said the *London City Mission Magazine* in 1845.[21] Another pastor reported that in poor neighborhoods "brazen, ragged women scream and shout ribald repartees from window to window."[22] Meanwhile, upper class women advertised their blue blood by cloistering themselves inside — not opening their doors until the Second World War. (In reality, the 'commoners' had standards of sexual behavior similar to the upper classes, writes Françoise Barret-Ducrocq in her study of 19th century British sexual mores. Lower-class women expected to be courted and sexual intercourse was seen as a prelude to marriage. Most men kept up their end of the bargain.)

Chastity has always had its opponents. A woman who loses her virginity before marriage "imagines she cannot fall lower," wrote Mary Wollestonecraft in the 18th century, but the world which proscribes this, she continued, reduces women to the "observance of one virtue."[23] Hundreds of year later, teenage girls will still not have sex with their boyfriends for fear of the stigma should anyone find out. One study of teenagers showed that while they engage in every other manner of sexual behavior, sex is déclassé. Standards of what makes a slut change, but the label sticks. When I was in high school over a decade ago, a girl showing up with a bare midriff and hip-hugger pants would have been instantly considered the school slut. Now no one blinks at that uniform. Adult women don't have it any better.

Newspaper articles advise not sleeping with a man for four months, or until he has said he loves you. A young British lawyer became known around the world after he forwarded an e-mail from his girlfriend, Claire, to his male buddies. And when Brad the Cad's friends saw it, they felt compelled to show it to five friends, who showed it to five friends and so on, so that by December of 2000, the names of both Brad and Claire were known around the world. Claire was in hiding.

Like this we police ourselves. Bombarded with the message that their value resides in their sexual attractiveness, Western women learn to exercise power by withholding sex. It's a tricky game to win. For some reason, the current times are particularly angry at women's sexuality and our shadow slut particularly fierce. Listen to Britney Spears' avowals of her chastity. A teenaged nymph whose siren call is answered by young and old men alike (it was a businessman who offered the singer $17-million to sleep with him, not a 10-year-old fan), Spears feels compelled to proclaim loudly that she wants to keep her virginity until marriage.

Spears, or her managers, understand what is at stake. She is allowed to inflame desire, indeed she must do so to keep up her record sales, but any desires of her own must remain well hidden, lest she be thought trashy and her adoring fans turn into a revolted and revulsed mob. Far from being a powerful role model for ambitious young women, Britney's look-but-don't-even-think-of-touching strategy is just the latest way to keep girls confused; always looking pretty but always passive, ashamed of what they want and feel. The problem is not that Spears says she wants to remain a virgin until her wedding night, it's that her declaration of purity is held up as evidence that though to unclean minds she might look like a whore, she's really the Madonna. Spears can't veer from her course as a precious commodity — her most marketable asset is that she exists in this no-man's land between those two hoary archetypes, between what her look says and her innocence.

Woe be to those who don't know how to inhabit this slippery ground. Lean too much to one side and you're loose, too much to the other, a nerd. "Girls," says Peggy Orenstein in her study of adolescent self-esteem, *Schoolgirls*, "learn to stand outside of themselves, to disconnect and evaluate themselves as others might. As they mature, then, the question they begin to ask themselves is not whether they desire (a notion they quickly suppress) but whether or not someone would desire them."[24] Young girls just discovering their sexuality are flooded with conflicting messages about how they are supposed to behave. The only pressure boys face is to do it, but no one thinks to call the high-school charmer a slut. What's missing from this picture, Orenstein says, is girls' own desire — a subjugation of their pleasure to societal mores that is the first step to ensnaring their selves for a long time to come.

After grade seven comes grade eight and after that grade nine. As a child, I have numerous pictures of myself frolicking around the beach naked. On a family trip when I was 15, my mother decided to run around nude on a deserted beach. I was encouraged to do the same. I was mortified and of course, declined. The next year, however, as I grew breasts and started smelling funny sometimes and was spending more time than usual in my room brooding over boys, I would incur the wrath of both my parents for wearing short skirts. The problem wasn't so much what I looked like in a short skirt — like a skinny 16-year-old — but that I was sending out signals I was available. Not being a parent myself, I don't know what I would do. I like to think I would let my daughter do whatever she wants, but probably I won't. Probably I'll feel the need to make sure she's showing off her flat stomach or long legs or wears shirts cut too low because she is confident in her sexuality not because of peer pressure. (Every family has its own circus performance.)

As a teenager, I left the house looking perfectly nerdy in loose pants, long skirts, baggy shirt. Within 45 minutes, I would arrive at my best friend's house, borrow one of her short skirts, throw on a pair of black tights and put on her black, short lace-up boots. Then I'd put on make-up, eyeliner, and eye shadow. The whole outfit would be changed again at the end of the day. When I'm on the subway now and I see flanks of girls dressed in identical revealing clothing I know it all comes from one of their closets.

Yet I, and these teenage girls, all wanted boys not just to desire us, but also to respect us, listen to us, love us. In one episode of the long-defunct TV series *My So-Called Life*, the school slut finds out everyone thinks she's "easy." Out go the flashy clothes, the green eye shadow, and the teased hair. In come the long, demure skirts, the blazers, and the pearls.

The funny thing about being a slut is that much as a slut is derided, she is admired. A slut has a lot more fun. The teenaged slut goes out on dates all the time and is pursued by boys; the adult slut has a similar life, her phone ringing off the hook with all the men she's met during her latest outing at a bar or a party. In a world where women are trained to desire male attention, trained to attract and keep it, and given remedial lessons on the cover of every magazine available at the checkout counter, the slut looks like the girl who aced the exam. The same magazines also advise women on how not to seem too easy, "how to keep his interest." How to be sexy, but not sluttish; fascinating and mysterious and not too available. Women learn to watch that they don't step on the cracks.

Should they fail to keep the balance they have only to look to Monica Lewinsky to see their fate. Lewinsky's long conversations with Linda Tripp were really just attempts to convince herself that she was more to Bill than just a woman for his convenience, more than just a slut who'd signaled her availability by showing him her thong. Selling handbags on the Internet and being referred to as "that woman" does not really appeal to most of us as the finale to the end of an affair. No one would think to mistake Monica for Helen of Troy and yet why not? Both women caused powerful men to risk everything, and I'd like to believe that only lusty, carnal women would provoke those emotions in their men.

That day is far off. The only women who are called sluts as a compliment are porn stars. And even these women, who have arguably made careers out of being sluts, feel they have to justify their choices. "It was a piss-take on the whole notion of masculinity," says Annabel Chong, the first porn actress to set a gang-bang record in 1995 by supposedly having sex with 251 men in 10 hours. Chong, who has a master's degree in gender studies at the University of Southern California and is now directing porn films for women, explains that the X-rated movie made of her stunt was a way for her "to take on the role of a stud."[25]

"I just wanted to do something that was obviously the opposite of what nice girls are supposed to do,"[26] she said later. Would a man have to explain why he showed up for the shoot?

Chong was only the first, though. After her, Jasmin St. Claire broke the record with 300 men. Others followed. In every instance, men traveled from across the U.S. for the chance to have sex with a porn star for two minutes while other men watched. I don't know if these men would marry these women, but they certainly would kill their daughters if they made career choices similar to the those of the women they came to have a go at.

In the 1995 movie *Chasing Amy*, the lead character falls for Amy and in a plot that defies belief turns the lesbian heroine into a man-loving vixen. Their relationship is not undone by her bisexuality, or by the disapproving frowns of her friends. It ends after Amy's revelation that in high school she had sex with two boys at the same time and enjoyed it. She has no interest in repeating the experience, but in the guy's mind, she has fallen from her pedestal. No longer the trophy he'd fought for and won, she's now just used goods.

When I was single a few years ago, I would spend every Saturday night going out dancing with my female friends. My skirts were a lot shorter than they were in high school, but I was still not meeting anyone I would want to date though I was pretty pleased with what I finally looked like. It struck me then how irrelevant the word slut truly was. The point wasn't how I looked to others, it was how they looked to me, and how I looked to myself.

The knots we twist ourselves into affect the intimate relationships of every woman. Funnily enough, the same society which limits women's acceptable behavior is aware of the effects. A 1938 marriage manual advised husbands that their new brides may be a bit reluctant to have sex at first. "She has all her life been taught that the one thing she must not do is surrender to any man, and she cannot, in every case, cast off the effects of this teaching in a moment."[27] The flipside of branding women as sluts is the necessity of repressing their sexual potential, even from themselves.

As early as 1559, Venetian scientist Renaldus Columbus named the clitoris "the love or sweetness of Venus," going on to advise rubbing it to give a woman pleasure. For two hundred years after, a commonly held view was that women could not conceive without having an orgasm; and so women's orgasms were paramount. Physicians advised that women who experienced difficulty becoming pregnant "be titillated before intercourse."[28] In 1850, as women were beginning to whisper about getting the vote, *The Westminster Review* pronounced desire in women "dormant, if not non-existent."[29] In 1886, the publication of the influential *Psychopathia Sexualis* by Richard von Krafft-Ebing, the first book to categorize sado-masochism, decreed that women who were excessively horny were nymphomaniacs.

Then things got better again. In 1899, Havelock Ellis argued that women could orgasm and by 1902, U.S. physician Elizabeth Blackwell wrote that women had as "unbridled [an] impulse of physical lust"[30] as men. Doctor and birth control advocate Marie Carmichael Stopes expanded on the theme: she admonished husbands to make sure their wives are ready for intercourse, explaining that women's sexual responses are "so complex, so profound . . . that in rousing them the man is rousing her whole body and soul."[31]

In the 21st century, the sexually-responsive woman is embraced by third- and fourth-wave sex-positive feminists wearing t-shirts proclaiming they are a "rock slut," sleeping with whomever they want, whenever they want (or not). These are women like the editors of New York-based *Bust* magazine who include at least one or two light, celebratory essays by women on sex in every issue. "Wear comfortable clothes. How can you be 'in the mood' when you're hobbling down the street in heels with your underwear riding up your butt?" says

Lady J in one article. "Skip one expendable girlie activity a day. Instead, use that time to masturbate."[32]

Another woman captures the confusion of discovering that what turns you on is the very thing that is forbidden. "Benta gets everything," writes Lisa Palac of the feeling that overcame her the first time she read an S/M story. "Tied up, whipped, fingered . . . She ends up having a couple of great big orgasms, and when it's all over she is worshipped with kisses by everyone. My guilty conscience arrived right on time, whispering, that's bad. How could any woman want such things? I wanted so badly to be Benta."[33]

Some women have always gotten away with being Benta, or at least with owning up to that side of themselves. Mae West was the first modern Benta. Singing *A Guy What Takes His Time* in *She Done Him Wrong*, West was a lusty she-devil, asking for what she wanted with a thrill that transcended the screen and put fear in the hearts of moral crusaders. Censors came up with the Hays Code, in which actors had to keep one foot on the ground when kissing, as a way to save America from West's lewd influence. Decades later, we've been spell (and sales) bound by Madonna, and more recently Angelina Jolie, she of the big lips and ever-present cigarettes. Like West, these women have to be put in their place sometimes. Madonna has never been more loved than when she married director Guy Ritchie in a modern, super-wealthy twist on a traditional wedding in a Scottish castle. The wedding dress may have been designed by Stella McCartney, but a wedding dress it was and it wiped clean years of debauchery. And Jolie? A kiss and proclamation of love for her brother at the 1999 Oscar ceremonies where she won an Oscar for *Girl, Interrupted*, led to a frenzy of media speculation that she was unstable.

If even famous girls are more loved when they're good, for the not famous among us, being bad feels good, but it does nothing for our rep. To say to a woman that she is a slut is perhaps one of the most powerful insults you can hurl at her. It implies she is desperate and willing to be disposable, has no self-respect and is treating her sexual self without care. Boys who knowingly go out with sluts hoping to get laid are astounded when these girls turn them down or say no. As a friend of mine said once, "Men don't understand that just because you're interested in sex doesn't mean you don't want to fall in love."

One of the most common conversations women have goes something like this. One of the women has a date with a new man. She is very attracted to him. She also likes him and would like to investigate his views of matrimony and children during the course of the date. Then this . . .

"Do you think I should wait? I should wait, shouldn't I? They always say you should wait until the third date."

Over time, depending on the frequency of such conversations, the number of times a woman has broken up with a previous partner, her sexual experience, her emotional vulnerability, the responses vary. Mine have ranged from "It's not so hard to wait. I mean it is. But you can do it. You'll savor the moment more," to "Oh, who cares," to the most recent, which is "Who exactly is *they*?"

The *they* is not just men whose infamous ability to not pick up the phone is attributed to already having got some, but all the people we've ever talked to who've been burned and all the books promising no more burns. Is it good to wait? Yes. But only because it offers the illusion of emotional safety. A much more logical test would be to sleep with a man on the first date, if we were so inclined, and then if he were to not call, assume he is a swine and move on. After all, the callers would be the ones who having gotten the milk would still like to have evenings of conversation. The most reasonable alternative would be not to care. But I don't know anyone who doesn't.

The standards change all the time. That's the essence of power — if they didn't, women might gain some control of what they want to do and with whom without being afraid. Nobody wants to see herself not so gently ushered to the seats in the "slut" section. The consequences can be nasty. One of my best friends in my teenage years was considered a slut. She was also the sweetest girl I knew, once suffering through a long rendition of the dance scene in *Flashdance*, complete with falling-down leg warmers, which I performed in my bedroom. I think she applauded before advising me to stop watching every rerun of *Fame*. We lost touch for many years until I ran into her at a subway station when I was 19. The long black hair that had earned her the reputation was gone and the curves had turned into a weight problem. Holding on to each of her hands were two pre-schoolers. Both hers. Continuing her education was out of the question. What would have happened to this girl if having a lot of boyfriends in high school did not carry a stigma; if she had been told she can do what she wants as long as she keeps up her grades? I'd argue that she would have worried less about how to keep her partners interested and more about her own life. Boys come upon tales of men ruined by women almost by accident — say, if they happen to read *Of Human Bondage* or Nabokov's *Laughter in the Dark* — but girls are taught that boys can ruin them almost as soon as they can speak. Much as I think all adolescent sexuality should be protected and savored, I also think there is a risk of making teenagers too preoccupied with their sexual selves. I've never been one to be able to walk away from someone I've been intimate with, but I think it's a good quality to have at times. No one is defined solely by who they bedded last night. No one except the slut.

The consequences of being this woman are not just semantic and not just damaging to a woman's sexual future. Sexual looseness is so condemned that it can lead a woman to a life of hardship. Canada's so-called rape shield law was a direct response to the efforts of lawyers for the accused to paint the woman who laid charges of rape as sexually loose. Invoking an accuser's sexual past is now rarely permissible evidence. If it's no longer OK to rape a slut, it's still OK to make her poor. As the essayist and activist June Jordan points out, decades of stigmatizing births to African-American women have led to real economic fallout. Like the friend I encountered at the subway, they have been punished by a social system which brands them immoral. Social assistance cuts, inadequate day care, exorbitant health care costs, none would not be tolerated in a country where women's sexuality is private, not fodder for political games in which a country cheers when "bad girls" are made to pay for their supposed recklessness.

I draw some solace from seeing women get mad at being forced into such boxes. Whatever will be said about former U.S. President Bill Clinton, he seems to like his women fiery. When he crosses them, they get very pissed off. Paula Jones: raised in a strict religious home, her hemlines monitored by her parents, she quickly transformed herself into a superslut after the death of her father, a member of the Bible Missionary Church. As one journalist reported, her skirts "shot up the thighs," she painted her nails red, permed her hair, and wore blue eye shadow. A few years later, what happens? No one is yet entirely clear whether Clinton really asked her to perform oral sex, but at the very least she probably caught his eye and not because he wanted to date her. I'm not that kind of girl, Jones says later, and tries to launch a sexual harassment suit.

Jones doesn't have much credibility these days, what with her pictorial in *Penthouse* last year confirming her rep. But from the beginning of her notoriety, all Jones was asking for was a little respect. As she put it in a 1994 press appearance, "I don't have no credentials, no law degree like Anita Hill,"[34] but that doesn't mean you should laugh at me.

Ironically, some argue that in the end it's the slut who is best equipped for love. In the book inspired by her own ostracization as a slut in high school, Leora Tanenbaum says after the wounds healed and she grew up, she realized that she and the women she interviews in *Slut!* were ahead. Sluts, she writes, "recognize that most girls take adolescence romance much more seriously than boys do — too seriously. Seriously active 'sluts' think of themselves as independent sexual agents and are less inclined to use sex as a bargaining chip for love and affection."[35]

My personality has generally prevented me from behaving in the way a slut is supposed to behave. Whether through conditioning or genetics, I tend to form strong attachments to the people I have had sex with; when that has not happened it has provoked a crisis of self. Quite probably I am afraid of finding out what it would be like to have anonymous sex all the time, afraid I might like it, afraid I might find myself exiled from emotional communion and not miss it. I have no idea what I would be like had I grown up in a hypothetical society where sex for women was not polluted with a variety of negative images, where sexual enjoyment could be just that. I have always been envious of friends I've had who have said in passing that they were going to meet a new man for an evening and in response to my question as to whether they thought it might become something, shrugged and said they didn't want it to be. They just wanted "to get laid," to have a moment of physical and emotional union with someone they didn't know very well nor did they wish to know them. I can't do it and I'm sorry for that sometimes — for being unable to leave my thinking self behind and simply immerse myself in experience — but I am a product of the world I grew up in and it's pointless for me to try. All I would get is a nervous breakdown.

As in high school, women who embrace the bad girl inside inspire me. They are Mary Magdalene and Scherezade, plucking themselves out of the sexual obscurity into which they have been cast and spinning their own stories. They are shameless, in love with their sexual selves in whatever form they might emerge. I'll always be the girl who looks on from the sidelines at the girls in tight sweaters and tighter jeans and wonders exactly how they got their red nail polish to look flawless when I know they bought the same pot of $1.99 enamel I have at home. These women live outside the confines imposed on them. Every day they break the rules without regard for the consequences because they do not recognize any authority that brands a woman "a slut" and then punishes her for acts no one ever asked her if she thought were immoral.

CHAPTER **FIVE**

A MIDSUMMER'S NIGHT DREAM

I went to the Pussy Palace on a mid-summer evening. The building where the event was held is normally a gay men's bathhouse and next to it is a Toronto hotel with rooms overlooking the bathhouse's pool. The view out-of-towners got must have been tremendous, but this is better. The view from the inside. If Shakespeare were alive, and had he attended, he may have been persuaded to dedicate his own summer dream to the event.

Fifty to 60 women are lounging around a pool. Some are eating dips and veggies, some are getting their bodies painted, some are playing charades. Many of the women aren't wearing much. Among the ones who are still dressed, some have opted for leather vests and kilts, others for frilly, short nightgowns, one for a fishnet, body-hugging dress and yet another for a white tulle princess skirt.

"Women don't express our desire to just have sex, not to move in, not to love each other, but just to have sex," Loralee, one of the event's organizers tells me. "We are socialized to not own our desires. The bathhouse challenges that. We're all here because we're horny."

And she's right: for 12 hours I found myself at an X-rated Lilith Fair with 200 other women. Sometimes it seems the only things girls need to be transformed into sluts is a hot night, a welcoming house and lots of other uninhibited girls. I think of that night as a walk on the wild side of female sexuality, of what women are capable of and of how open they can be about their desires. Some of the girls there had come to simply socialize, to hang out with other women and have a drink, maybe flirt and eventually, should the mood strike them, set up a date for later. Others had come with partners, to drink in the atmosphere the way a straight couple might go to a dance club and spend all night rubbing up against each other. A frisson in public becoming fireworks in private.

4:30 p.m.: I line up with about 50 other women outside the club, all of us waiting to snap up the last batch of $15 tickets. A few days earlier, the 150 or so advance tickets sold in just over an hour.

One woman walks up and down the line offering everyone strawberries she had picked that morning from a farm outside the city. Other women are discussing their master's theses in sociology or women's studies. A woman with long, dark hair, sharp features, and deep, red lipstick is telling a slightly older woman all about how she wants to become a filmmaker.

It turns out the older woman, Emily, works in the film industry. She proceeds to advise her newfound friend on different ways to get into the movie business. Emily has brought an overstuffed backpack, a shoulder bag, and a family-sized cooler.

"What's in the cooler?" someone asks her.

"Ice," she says. Then she adds, "Ice can be a sex toy. The flyer said BYO-TOYS."

At the front of this bathhouse, the managers have posted a notice to the regular patrons. It explains that "ladies" will be taking over the club for the evening and it will therefore be closed to the male patrons. Then, its last two lines read, "We apologize for the inconvenience." Last time I heard women called "ladies" was at a Puff Daddy show, as in "how would you ladies like to come up here? How about that, hmm?"

I read the notice on my way in and though I frown at it, it also makes me feel more daring for going in. The rest of the walls are postered with safe sex ads and announcements about reduced prices on yearly memberships.

The box-office, as it were, is behind an iron cage. On the wall above the clerk plays a lesbian porn tape, a cowgirl at a rodeo at night being sodomized by a group of other women. This first glimpse is both promising and menacing but mostly it's saying "make no mistake about it, you are entering nasty zone."

6 p.m.: I get back home, make some dinner and organize the little party that will go to the bathhouse in a couple of hours. Earlier in the week, I had arranged with a friend to go with another couple of people. The day of, I have second thoughts. I am friends with the woman, but not good friends, while at the same time I have known her for about a decade. I realize I do not want to know if she will have sex tonight, that kind of information crossing a boundary in our loose friendship that would bond us beyond the limits we have imposed thus far. Already, like a girl, I am analyzing what is supposed to be an evening of no-strings-attached sex, this even though I'm not planning to have any myself. I call newer friends.

So our little group ends up looking like this: me, my friend, Anna, Rosalee, Andrea and Jennifer representing a variety of sexualities from hetero to poly.

All the women worry about whether or not they are attractive enough, whether their clothes are appropriate. I'm wearing what has become my summer uniform of capri pants and white, sleeveless t-shirt and am thankful I'm not looking to get picked up because in this sporty outfit I figure my chances aren't great. We're going to a women's-only space and from what I remember from my university days we're not supposed to be worrying about how we look. As if.

Rosalee is a volunteer stripper for the evening. She's gone to classes teaching her how to arouse and tease the person she's dancing for, how to say no to touching, or how to say yes if she happens to like the girl and they want to meet in a private room. As a dancer, she's been given a private room to store her gear. She's decked out in a PVC dress with garters and we all crowd into the room and admire her outfit. Unfortunately, one of the garters is broken and though we all take turns trying to fix it, it doesn't work. She swears and stomps around in a most unladylike fashion and eventually decides to go garterless. Anna is going for the butch look: army shorts and a tight black tank top. Andrea and Jennifer are wearing street clothes, jeans, and t-shirts. Everyone keeps moaning about how none of us are stylish enough; we've done it to ourselves, toning down our normal fashion sense as if being somewhat dowdy will protect us from the sexual charge in the air.

Still, the women's worries are not just related to our gender. Later on, when I do some research on the history of the gay male bathhouse, I realize that far from always being the hedonistic havens we think of, the gay bathhouse can also be a cauldron of insecurities, resembling the elementary school ritual of humiliation otherwise known as picking members of a sports team.

The nudity of the gay bathhouse is supposed to make everyone equal.[36] Naked, there are no Rolex watches or expensive suits to give away how much money someone makes, nor any shabby shoes to reveal how little someone else makes either. You're picking based on the quality of the flab (and perhaps the quality of the conversation) alone. In reality, though, lots of men are rejected over the course of any night for not being buff enough, not being handsome enough, or for being too old. Men over 45 are often looked at as dirty old men. Stripped of their clothes, they are also stripped of their social status, their worth reduced to just how they look naked.[37]

Women are supposed to be more egalitarian, but as a female friend of mine maintains, the reality is different. Women dress for and want to impress each other. And as the night wears on at the Pussy Palace, those who are less attractive are left on the sidelines.

At one point, I talk to a woman who came to the bathhouse by herself all the way from Hamilton, about an hour away from Toronto. She's black, very pretty, but heavier than she would like. She has a towel knotted around her waist. She is a painter. She likes painting nude female bodies, she says softly as she watches women mill about naked around the pool. When I come back from wandering around for about an hour or so she is still sitting alone against the far wall of the pool deck.

10 p.m.: The heat from the downstairs steam room and whirlpool rises and gives the four-storey house a musty, hot smell that seems to creep and cling to the walls of the narrow, dimly lit hallways. A dry and hot sauna, whirlpool, and showers are in the basement.

The second floor has an S/M demonstration room outfitted with mirrored walls and exercise equipment to which women will be tied and sometimes whipped over the course of the evening. A bar and lounge area and two hallways of private rooms take up the rest of the floor.

The third floor houses a large-screen TV that plays explicit hard-core lesbian porn the whole night. It also has the Temple Priestess room, run by Leanne, who offers free "touch healing" sessions, a few private rooms, a group sex room, and a porn photo room where women can get dirty pictures taken of themselves.

The fourth floor is almost entirely taken up by private rooms, except for two hallways. The first leads to a fire escape and has a bench running along the whole length of the wall. In this hallway, women who have volunteered to be strippers and lap dancers will perform while their "clients" will sit on the bench. The second hallway seems to serve no particular purpose. It also also has a room-length bench along one wall. A mirror covers the entire wall opposite.

For much of the night, I walk around the house, peering into rooms with the doors open, watching women fix their make-up or their clothes in the bathrooms, marveling at the constantly impassable crowd watching the going-ons in the S/M demonstration room, waiting to see if the group sex room will ever actually become a group sex room or whether it will remain empty all night (it is in use, but very, very seldom), and exchanging friendly, flirtatious glances with the women lined up at the make-shift bar.

It is only by morning, however, that I begin to have some idea of how to navigate my way around the house without getting lost. The lay-out, I figure, with back staircases, hallways leading to dead ends and implausibly placed bathrooms, is designed to maximize the potential for anonymous, spontaneous encounters lasting five to ten minutes.

The expression on our faces is similar. Especially early on in the evening. It's almost a childlike pleasure in finding ourselves in this house, a "Hey, Ma, I'm on TV" look that we exchange with each other. Five minutes in here and even Pollyanna would feel the bad girl within stirring and because we all feel this, we feel bad and we like it. I do anyway, a lot.

Rosalee has asked Anna and I if we want to go watch her strip for a woman. We agree and sit down on a couple of chairs behind Rosalee. The woman she is dancing for is a butch, in green army pants and a black gas station attendant's shirt. She has short, buzzed hair. She also has a sweet face and is shy so that when Rosalee starts unzipping her dress, she first looks away, then looks back, then looks away again.

I've been to straight strip clubs, in fact to about four or five or them in the few weeks before the bathhouse night. I've gone in the name of research with a female friend who is writing a novel about a stripper. Where those women dance in ways that understandably are designed to preserve their energy, Rosalee's dance is much, much better. I tell Anna that unlike the pros, Rosalee looks like she is genuinely enjoying herself. Also because she is enjoying herself and clearly straining in some of her moves to be as much of a dancer as she can accomplish, she looks real. She looks, in other words, like a woman who is dancing for a lover or trying to seduce a potential one. (Indeed, the woman on the bench when we watch Rosalee will be one of her many conquests for the evening.)

"Was it OK, you guys? What did you think, what did you think?" Rosalee says when she finishes. We both tell her how good she was. Later on, when I talk to her about the whole experience, she says she found it fulfilling beyond her wildest expectations, not least because it gave her power.

"I've been that powerless around someone, because they make

you so hot, you know," she says. "I liked watching the women I was dancing for, seeing them turned on, seeing the effect my work had on them. The butches tried to hide it, but they couldn't.

"With anything that's erotic, there's always the risk you'll fail, that you'll fail to turn someone on. I was scared that would happen but it didn't. I turned them all on."

Whole hours seem to pass by in the bathhouse with nothing happening. Anna and I wander around aimlessly. Anna talks about whether she should really try and pick up a woman, seeing as she has a boyfriend waiting at home, even though her boyfriend has agreed to her sleeping with a woman. What he's told her is that he does not own her body, a statement that the bathhouse organizers would surely approve. A woman's body at this bathhouse is hers alone, and only hers to offer, a political sentiment perhaps best expressed in what's called the Cupid Game.

The Cupid Game has turned everyone sitting in the pool area into an instant Cyrano de Bergerac. Women who want to be picked up can have a number drawn in marker on their shoulders. Once someone has seen an object of lust they walk over to a table covered in pink flyers. The flyers have several categories the writer can fill in, including a description of the writer (horny, submissive, wet, etc.), a description of the writee (similar to the writer), and various activities and body parts the writer is interested in from kissing to spanking, from eyes to ass. The sheet filled in, you post it on a bulletin board with the person's number on the back and your own number — should they wish to find you — on the front.

At any one time, about 100 women now mill around the edges of the pool. The bulletin board, however, has at most 20 or 25 messages on it and is constantly swarmed by women hoping someone has seen them. Watching everyone obsessively check the board for their numbers reminds me of staring at the phone willing it to ring with someone else on the other line but the usual suspects.

The friends I'm with aren't getting any messages at all. Neither is a very pretty, blond woman who has come by herself and is now sitting with us, too shy to go mingle. They all begin to descend into a sullen silence punctuated by moans of "No one likes me." I grab a bunch of flyers and write messages to everyone and go post them on the board. After a pretend span of time, I go retrieve the messages I wrote and hand them out. It hardly matters that everyone knows I wrote them, the mood brightens.

The bathhouse is all about desire, not just having it for someone else but also feeling desired. The chances of both of those things happening aren't bad, but they are not certain, and when the women here don't feel desired the shock to their self-esteem is not shielded by years of experiencing rejection, the way, say, a gay male who goes to a bathhouse a couple of times a week might take it. In this "sex-positive" environment, the Cupid Game is both flirtation and danger. The danger is in not being picked and really, in not having sex. Paradoxically, the organizers came up with the game for women who will not necessarily have sex. "We wanted to have different ways to participate," Loralee says. "The Cupid Game was part of that. At least half the women don't have sex, but they want to be there."

The organizers are also aware, however, of the potential for rejection. Leanne, who describes herself as a spiritual sex goddess — another name for a professional sex therapist — is busy all night.

"The bathhouse allows people to explore their feelings without financial or emotional punishment," she says. "But it's still emotionally risky. With me, they are released from complications and obligations."

"Sex is power and it can turn if you're not careful."

12:00 p.m.: The porn on the TV has changed from the softcorish of the early night, a woman giving another woman a massage, to hardcore S/M. In the straight world, women are renting more and more porn, either to watch alone or with a partner. Regardless of the numbers, though, a woman who says she watches porn is still saying she's open to trying something different.

Well, imagine a room full of mostly naked women drinking beer and sitting on bleacher-style seats in front of a large screen TV. All are completely silent, absorbed in images of a woman being burnt with hot wax. Funny thing is, the scene sounds erotic, but it's not. They might be watching it together, but each viewer is deep in her own private reverie. Still, by this time, the porn viewing room has become known as the place to pick-up, probably because everyone in it is already naked.

1:00 a.m.: Every few minutes another woman strips off her clothes and dives into the pool. It's the fastest way to signal one's availability. As would be the case at a bar, or in day-to-day life, the women who are not taking off their clothes are the most coveted. All night, everyone has been eyeing a Julie Andrews look-alike, covered head-to-toe in jeans and a long-sleeved t-shirt. Women venture to talk to her and then give up. Every hour, she is chatting with someone new. She has a charming smile and seems friendly, but from the fact that she never leaves the pool area, it's clear she will not put out for anyone tonight.

The other tease is a couple, one of the women a dead ringer for Katie Holmes (Joey Potter in *Dawson's Creek*), the other tall and skinny with long, blue hair. The whole pool area watches as they both go and get numbers drawn on their shoulders. Then they find a quiet corner where the blue-haired half proceeds to do a lap dance for her partner.

Our table decides to write them a message which I am sent to post. When I post it on the board, I see several other women have beaten us: several pink flyers with the couple's number on the back are already on the board. A little while later, the two go and retrieve their love notes and read them. They laugh as they open each one, then walk out hand in hand. You can almost hear the sound of jaws dropping when they make their triumphant exit.

2:00 a.m.: Women who got there early enough in the evening could book a room. The decor is strictly prison-chic. A single bed sits against a wall and a mirror runs along the bed. Next to the bed, a tall metal closet and a night table take up most of the rest of the space. The only extravagance is a dimmer light switch.

In the rooms all the resonances of the word "bathhouse" are alive. After the beginning of the AIDS epidemic and the busts of bathhouses and public washrooms in New York and San Francisco, public sex among gay men declined. The memory of it, however, was so powerful that artists have attempted to capture it. New York photographer Tony Just saw the demise of public sex as symbolic of the end of an era and eulogized the overwhelming feeling of sex in photos of public washrooms that had once served as unofficial meeting places for gay men but had been cleaned up by the city's authorities.

What these artists were trying to convey is this. In the rooms, the fuzzy feelings that float through the rest of the house are absent. When you walk in, there is no mistaking what the purpose of the room is, or what happens there several times a night. Before going into a room, men use a variety of signals to indicate what they are looking for. The way a towel is arranged on a man's body indicates which part of his body he wants most attention paid to; complementary towel-wearers get together.[38] Once inside the room the deciphering of such signs ends and the intimacy of walking into someone's bedroom for the first time takes over. Except it's magnified because there has never been any doubt about either partner's intentions.

Later on, I talk to Sandra, a woman who has gone to one other lesbian bathhouse before. She was explicitly drawn to it by the mystique of the gay tradition. Once inside, she took her cue from them as well.

"I enjoyed finding a room and leaving the door open and seeing how readily women would drop by. There were a number who did," she says.

Sandra did not go as far as men do. Still, she is a bit unusual in being so frank about what she wanted. She's always been fascinated by the world of public sex, she says, and has gone to underwear parties, parties where women strip down and what follows is up to the imagination.

3:00 a.m.: By this time, almost all of the doors to the rooms are closed. I walk around the hallways and guiltily listen to what's happening inside. On the third floor, in one room, a woman is whispering to her partner. From another, come the sounds of a whip being wielded. On the fourth floor hallway, all the doors are closed and the sound seeps out from under the doorways. The hallway is ringing with the sounds of women in the middle of having sex.

I have never heard such a thing, outside of hearing it on the soundtrack of porn movies. I try and explain the peculiar sense of excitement and liberation I feel at that moment to friends later, but whether they're women or men they don't seem to quite get it. Everyone who went to the bathhouse remarks on it later, though.

"It was amazing, wasn't it?" Loralee says when I ask her if she heard the same things I did.

Rosalee just grins and says, "Oh, I know, I know. Awesome."

Maybe it's this. No matter how many self-help books on sexuality a woman reads or how understanding her partner is, for many women sex does have moments of uncomfortability, perhaps with our own vulnerability. Making noise during sex, sounding like a slut, is an expression of this, it's letting the other person know exactly how they're making you feel. You can go to Annie Sprinkle's orgasm seminars until you're blue in the face, but nothing fuels one's own desires as much as a chorus of women's voices actually letting loose.

3:30 a.m.: Nothing can also beat the scenes I witness next. I am told later that at the first bathhouse women were having sex on the outside fire escape, a whole string of women joined together from the third-storey landing to the bottom of the stairs at the edge of the pool. Still, I wasn't there. For this I am.

On a couch by the now closed bar a woman is having sex with three other women in a fashion that much resembles what was on the porn tapes in the TV room. She is in ecstasy.

I walk upstairs. Three women in the TV room are masturbating. On the long bench in the mirrored hallway on the fourth floor, two women are having sex in front of the mirror.

I know where I am and all but still, this defies and exceeds my expectations.

4:00 a.m.: Anna and Jennifer and Andrea have all gone home after not scoring. Exhausted, I would also like to head out except that Rosalee has given me her room keys while she is visiting another woman in her room. And now, Rosalee is missing somewhere behind the closed doors. The bathhouse is supposed to close now, but the organizers aren't going to kick anyone out until 5.

I go and sit outside on a bench by the pool. A woman in a short kilt and a leather vest comes over with her friend and asks me if I had a good time.

"Yeah, it was great," I tell her.

We talk for a while and I tell her whom I'm waiting for.

"Oh, she was a dancer, wasn't she?" her friend says.

"Yeah, she was great too," I say.

"I really like her. I think I'll wait with you," the woman says.

We sit there, silently, and look at the pool still shrouded in darkness. Women begin to trickle out of the rooms. Eventually our bench is crowded with about five or six of us. I mostly listen to them talk about the night they've had.

One of the women talks about "when [she] used to like boys."

"I used to go for these loser guys," she says, shaking her head.

"Remember how crazy I was about that guy?" she asks the friend sitting next to her. The friend looks heavenwards.

"That girl tonight, she's just like that guy," she says and frowns to herself.

5:00 a.m.: The first light of the sun shines off the empty pool. I'm still waiting for Rosalee. One of the women on the bench pulls out a bunch of Polaroids she had taken of herself and two friends in the porn photo room. The pics are very compromising but she says she's putting them on her fridge.

Another woman literally bounces over to the bench. She is waving a pair of women's black Calvin Klein boxer shorts in the air, a trophy.

"She was standing on the bed and wouldn't let me touch her but she took them off and just gave them to me," she says.

She passes the underwear around for the other girls to smell. "Isn't that wonderful?" she says. I have never seen a woman behave like this, nor a man — but then again I've never been around when men maybe pass around their girlfriend's panties to their buddies. The closest I've ever come is to present a boyfriend's t-shirt to a friend and encourage her to smell it for what at the time I found to be a heady scent of Player's cigarettes and boy sweat. I thought that would explain my obsession with this boy, but she politely declined. When the underwear reaches me, I smile at it and also politely decline.

Not that the girl cares or notices. "I'm going to go home and go to bed and not draw the blinds, just go to sleep with them on my head," she says.

I spot the woman who had brought the cooler full of ice standing a bit off. She looks slightly tired and somewhat dejected.

"So? Did you use up all your ice?" I ask her.

"Nah," she says, sighing.

"But you used up a little bit of the ice?"

She shrugs non-commitally.

"Well. There's always next time, right?" I tell her.

Just then, I finally see Rosalee.

"Oh man," are her first words.

"I have all your stuff. They wanted to clean your room," are mine.

"Oh man," she says again.

"You had a good time?" I ask her

"Oh yeah, oh yeah. These butches. I tell you," she says.

"Can we go home now? You can tell me in the cab," I say hopefully and we head out.

I talk to Rosalee a few weeks later about that night. In the end, she has kept in touch with a couple of the women she met that night. They have become casual, but steady, partners. I also find out something I didn't know, that Andrea and Jennifer met at the last bathhouse and have been together ever since. As the old joke about relationships between women goes, What do lesbians do on the second date? *Move in.*

When I told friends about the experience, a few were skeptical. Would I have felt the opportunity for women to meet other women anonymously and engage in sex, free to see or not see their partner again, would be as valuable if the bathhouse was heterosexual? What if instead of seeing what I saw — one woman sexually stimulated by three others at two in the morning in a darkened but public corner of the space — I'd seen one woman involved with three men? The short answer is no. I don't believe that we are so far along in our sexual politics that a woman can willingly choose to have anonymous sex with several men at the same time and not feel ashamed. In her mind, in her partners' minds even, the exchange may be solely one of pleasure and fulfilled fantasies. But as long as the culture all around us portrays women engaging in such activities as fallen, no woman can escape the psychological effects. It's obvious to point out that it is acceptable for a man to fantasize about having a harem of women at his sexual beck and call; when a woman does the same thing, it's still pathological.

Do I think all women everywhere fantasize about having anonymous sex at a bathhouse, by the way? No. As Daniel Reitz says about encounters between gay men, when you want "an occasional fuck . . . in a skanky room, it can be heaven on earth." When you don't want it and are still in that room, that's when "you're in trouble."[39] What I would like is for women to be able to make choices and face only those consequences that of their own making.

What the women's bathhouses provide is a temporary refuge, not a foolproof one, but one nonetheless, from these cultural pressures. For one night a couple of times a year, women can be as wild as they want without anyone judging them. It's a sexual utopia of a kind where each can choose her pleasure without fear of reprisals. So powerful is this vision — what the everyday world might look like if women were not walking around with a mental script of how their sexuality should be expressed — that soon enough it becomes threatening.

In late September of last year, another edition of Pussy Palace was invaded by five male police officers from Toronto's morality squad division. What they were doing there was unclear to everyone; in the end, two of the organizers were charged with serving liquor after hours. The officers themselves maybe did not know the true aim. Policing female sexuality happens all the time; this was just a very clear case of it. The political outcry was ferocious. This was not an unaware group of women, or one made up of women who were at all ashamed of what they were involved in. A picture of several of the women present at the bathhouse appeared in the national newspaper, *The Globe and Mail.* They were standing in a line, each of them with their arms crossed, all defiant. To take back women's sexuality from the billboards and the magazines and the porn films and the imaginations of everyone except for women themselves is not just an affirmation of women's right to their own pleasure, it's also a political action.

For the mainstream, the idea of women having casual sex is still not acceptable. Women have never had their own bathhouses. Despite the BYO-Toys advertisement on the back of the flyer promoting the night I attended, the front depicts a lovely photo of two women, dressed in lingerie, kissing each other. It's nice, but not too far from *Penthouse*'s two-girl pictorials.

So for a woman to go to a bathhouse is an act that as social theorists might say, is doubly, actually triply, transgressive. It doesn't matter if she really goes to have sex; in everyone's eyes that's why she's there. When I was locking my bike outside the line-up in the afternoon, a guy passed by and asked me what was going on.

"Is there a concert?" he said.

"No. They're trying to get tickets for a bathhouse."

He looked at me uncomprehending and his eyes were wide and horrified. For women, the shame of being a slut comes as Peggy Orenstein says, "not from actually having sex, but from thinking about it: from admitting desire."[40]

In the eyes of the world, all the girls lining up outside the bathhouse are whores, unashamed to be seen waiting for their desires to be fulfilled. Those same women are also directly participating in a gay community. This is true even if, as was the case with many women who were there that night, you are not out as a lesbian or a bisexual. Finally, while she becomes an explicit part of this community, she is also entering a realm that has been reserved for men. And unlike a woman going to a male strip club, say, not only is this woman simply entering a men's realm, she is taking it over.

When the organizers of the Pussy Palace first started looking for bathhouses, they in fact encountered resistance from managers.

"They asked us, Are you going to make a mess? Are you going to bleed over everything?" says Loralee.

The lesbian-oriented bathhouse is different from the gay bathhouse; the boys don't have the sweetness of the Cupid game. But the women at the lesbian bathhouse know all about the gay men who started the practice and the battles they waged. In the mind of the mainstream, gay bathhouses are free-for-alls, places where gay men go to have no-strings attached sex with dozens of other men. In the mythology of the gay community, bathhouses represent much more. Over the decades, they have also become political and social symbols in the fight for gay rights.

Much as women having group sex is now considered shameful, gay sex was not so long ago the love that dared not speak its name. In the 1950s, bathhouses like New York St. Marks' catered to families and immigrants during the day and gay men at night.[41] From the sixties to the early eighties, the gay bathhouse became a place of exuberant sexuality. Bette Midler, accompanied by Barry Manilow on piano, gave concerts at New York's Continental Baths; Hollywood released two bathhouse movies, *The Ritz* and *Saturday Night at the Baths;* and the managers offered their patrons Valentine's Day, Christmas, and New Year's Eve parties.[42] (The tradition continues to this day with Miss M look-alikes like Toronto's Kathy Thompson doing shows at local baths.[43]) In those early decades the baths were transformed from places where men had furtive sex, to places where they felt safe expressing their sexuality. In other words, they became spaces where community was created.

When they came under attack, that social aspect became political. In February 1981 police raided all six of Toronto's bathhouses. Men clad only in towels were taken outside in the middle of winter and questioned; others were lined up in the shower rooms and forced to submit to full-body cavity searches. Thousands of people protested in front of the police station and marched onto the provincial government's buildings attempting to break down the door. In the end, police convicted only one man out of about 300 they had arrested,[44] a track record that echoes the hours of police patrolling the hallways of the women's bathhouse only to emerge with a bunch of names and several liquor-licensing charges.

The battle over the baths was really galvanized at the beginning of the AIDS crisis in the mid-eighties when New York and San Francisco closed their baths. The uproar from the gay community invigorated a whole generation of gay activists. Some gay groups argued the bathhouses should adopt guidelines for safe sex, but no one wanted to see them closed. The bathhouses, activists argued, were the logical place for safe sex groups to distribute condoms and educate one of the groups most at risk of contracting the disease: gay men having casual, anonymous, and unprotected sex with each other.

The Christian Right flexed its muscle and mainstream America listened. "There is an arrogant community within the gay community. They will not allow you, as a city, to protect its citizens," said Cecil Butler, a Baptist minister, during the New York hearings to close the bathhouses.[45] The closings were a political move, seen by activists as the first step toward having anti-sodomy laws back on state law books. As Ron Najman, of the U.S. National Gay Task Force, told the *New York Native* weekly paper, while the closings appeared to target "sexual acts between gay men . . . they have not included vaginal intercourse [in the guidelines]."[46]

Since then, the bathhouses have reopened in all three cities, but AIDS has cast a pall over their attraction.

I knew one gay man who claims to frequent them but he spoke about going in guilty tones, partly because safe sex is still not always practised. The fear of police raids was replaced by the specter of death. Still, when Toronto police arrested several men at the Bijou movie theatre (which shows gay porn flicks) in the summer of 1999, gay advocates and gay media, like the gay newspaper *X-tra*, immediately wondered if the arrests were a sign that the police would go after the bathhouses again. As it turned out their concerns were right.

The same fear is responsible for the bathhouse organizers' trepidation at a version of this chapter that was to appear in *The Globe and Mail*. At the time, they begged me not to reveal all the goings-on just in case the police read the article and felt they had nothing better to do next time around — which is exactly what happened anyway. I agreed to their requests but in the end, the *Globe* was more interested in the Lilith, not the X-rated, bits anyway. The Cupid game was OK but the woman sniffing another woman's boxer shorts was cut out without any comment. It's a sentimental gesture, I protested. The cut stayed.

CHAPTER **SIX**

NATURAL WOMAN

In grade school, I was a tomboy. While my girlfriends' dolls were always perfectly coifed, their hair evidence of frequent brushing, mine had a bird's nest of different hairstyles, from braids to hacked off pigtails. While my girlfriends delighted in the shiny white leather shoes they wore to birthday parties to go with taffeta dresses, all I remember is hating the way my wool stockings felt against my legs. In school, girls wore a uniform of a shirt, tie, and skirt. As soon as I was home, I'd throw on a pair of pants or shorts and head for the park. I climbed trees, I rode my bike, I had races with the boys. I had very, very short hair. My mother said it looked "very French." There is a picture of me on my first day of school. Our uniforms included a hair band for the girls, with two big poofy ribbons on each side. On close-cropped hair this is still a look I'm hoping Alexander McQueen will adopt for his models. On a seven-year-old it looked bizarre.

Not until a good 15 years later did I finally understand Jean-Luc Godard was responsible for my shorn locks: Godard's *Breathless*, with its gamine, short blond-haired newspaper-peddling Jean Seberg, was released during my mother's early adolescence. It had a profound influence.

Stuck with the look, however, I made the most of it. Short hair does not get caught in trees and looks best with a pair of green military-style khakis. Short hair also means that when you're seven, people mistake you for a boy. Soon enough, I started acting like one as well, not least because I developed a habit of showing my adoration for various neighborhood boys by trying to become just like them.

The boys roller-skated really fast. So did I. The boys rode their bikes as if they were motorcycles, kicking up a storm of dust and pebbles and grit in the dirt when they braked. So did I. My knees bore the proof. I remember them always covered in just-healed-over wounds. In front of the other kids, I picked off the scabs and let rivulets of blood trickle down my legs. Never mind that I was a skinny, runt: I was a tough runt.

In junior high, when other girls were reading biographies of Pamela Des Barres, I was reading Jim Morrison's biography and wondering not just how come I had been so unlucky as to have been too young to see Morrison reportedly pull down his leather pants in 1969 Miami, but also what those leather pants would look like on me.

In my best friend's bedroom, a fantasy in pink (pink bedspread, pink canopy, pink dresser, off-white bureau), with books on the model Twiggy strewn around the bedroom floor, we would talk about two things: boys and what kind of band we'd start. She played piano and was teaching herself guitar; I was teaching myself a little guitar but liked the instant satisfaction of getting a nice, fat sound out of the bass strings without much practice. My memories of those days revolve around her in a green or blue face mask lounging on her bed painting her toenails, with me invariably lying on the floor, fiddling with the carpet and hypothesizing about what the lunch-time hello from one of the boys on my list could have meant.

"He likes you, OK?" she'd say. "OK," I'd say back, utterly unconvinced.

"What are you going to wear when we go on stage?" she'd ask.

"Black leather pants," I'd say, without a moment's hesitation.

"I'm going to wear that black stretch skirt I have, you know, the really short one," she'd say back.

"You can't play in that," I'd say, but of course she'd ignore me and jumping off the bed, open her closet and start finding outfits to try on for when she would become a rock star.

The summer when I turned 17, I got a job at a summer camp in Richmond Hill, a suburb about 10 kilometers outside of Toronto. I woke up at 7 in the morning (a hormone-driven bundle of energy), showered, threw on a pair of blue Levis, a red-and-white flowered bandanna to keep my (now longer) hair out of my eyes, and a short-sleeved red-and-green-and-white checkered shirt, then by 7:30 took my bike out of the garage and rode up the 10 kilometers. Every day I wore the same thing for the ride.

One time, on my way home, a downhill ride all the way that I gleefully made faster by pedaling at top speed, a car load of guys sped by, far too close to my red 12-speed Raleigh, the pride of my life, a machine I polished every other weekend and seriously described as part of my body.

"Hey baby," they yelled out, "you look like Springsteen."

At first I was proud, then I was mortified. I loved Bruce, but they hadn't exactly hit on me, more like hit on me then questioned my womanhood, man. Though I biked for many years after that, I think I lost something that day, as if my speed and my clothes — which were designed to keep me comfortable on the bike — were not compatible with getting a boyfriend. Of course I should not have cared, but this was the eighties and 17-year-olds weren't all feminists in the making.

A little later, I got one of those. A boyfriend, the same aforementioned one whose mother did his dumping for him. He'd seen me biking around the neighborhood, we'd made frequent eye contact, eventually I dismounted, said hello, and after asking each other's names, he asked me to a movie that night. A well-read hippie hash-head, he told me the secrets of life according to *Zen and the Art of Motorcycle Maintenance* while making me listen to Cat Stevens' *Tea for the Tillerman* and feeding me bacon-and-egg sandwiches in his room. He wore baggy army pants and baggy sweaters with a shirt on top of them and another lumberjack shirt on top of that. Underneath he had a skinny chest but large upper-arm muscles which I remember being able to feel even when he was in full combat gear.

We began looking a lot alike. Much as when I was a child with skinned knees, I had begun dressing like him. I liked it. In winter, it meant I could wear four layers and stay warm in cold weather, in summer it meant that I could wear baggy army shorts and a black, sleeveless t-shirt.

The image of the first girl I saw him with after we were no longer seeing each other is still imprinted on my brain: she was a wearing a long, loose flowing skirt and a purple, thin sweater. She also had straight hair all the way down to her waist. I don't know if I was more heartbroken about seeing him holding her hand or about the implicit rejection of me — and my look.

The guy after that liked the way I dressed at the time, but nevertheless over time the boy look faded. All that was left of it were a pair of scuffed cowboy boots I had for five years that made me feel as strong as riding a bike does, and then those hit the Goodwill box too.

What I've never lost, however, is the curiosity about what it would be like to be a man. *The Diagnostic and Statistical Manual* which lists all mental disorders, classifies a "persistent discomfort" about one's gender as gender dysphoria. I don't have "gender dysphoria," but on the odd day, I'd like to try being a man. There is the physical experience. What does an orgasm feel like for a man? What does it feel like to walk around with a penis? What does it feel like to touch a flat chest in the shower? Being male is not just a physical experience, it buys certain social allowances. (And forbids others.) The ability, say, to yell back at a stranger who verbally attacked me without being afraid of what they could do because I would know that because I was a man they feared me. The ability to sit on the streetcar or the subway with my legs spread out widely, taking up way more space than my fair share, taking up the other person's space, just because I could, because I would have a penis hanging between my legs, and dammit, it needs room. Or at least I imagine that that's what the stance implies.

Drag kings do it all the time. For me, one day would be enough. A life lived like the other, however, can exact the ultimate price, a life.

We love our outlaws. As long as they are up on a movie or TV screen,

Bonnie & Clyde blowing up banks, James Dean driving too fast, Janis Joplin playing too fast and singing too hard, Jim Morrison taking too many drugs and writing too much bad poetry. Them we make into pop culture icons, images on bedroom walls. Vicariously, we live all the lives we do not dare live ourselves. We want to be more, do more, but fear losing our families, our jobs, our neighborhoods, all the things that keep us grounded to ourselves should we risk actually living like this. All the outlaws die in the end. Those lucky enough to escape accidents, suicide, dissolution, all the turns of the fate to which they submit themselves so willingly, we demonize.

There has to be a price to pay for living outside the mainstream. If there isn't, if you can get away with being wild and doing as you please, with being who you want to be, then our own lives seem unnecessarily limited by comparison, steeped in quiet desperation. As readily as we build them up, we take down our heroes. That's what supermarket gossip tabloids are about — the lives we want and do not have in all their dirty glory. Thelma and Louise drive their car off the Grand Canyon because they cannot be allowed to make their own rules and live. Back when Courtney Love was still a hellion and not a Versace model with chemically peeled skin, it's why she was vilified.

One of the most fundamental ways in which we lead our lives is as men or women. "A woman shall not wear anything that pertains to a man, nor shall a man put on a woman's garment, for all who do so are an abomination to the Lord," says the Bible.[47] Every time a man becomes a woman, a woman a man, they dare society to justify why biology is destiny.

For most people New Year's Eve is a time to look back, take stock of the past year, look forward to the new one, make resolutions no one can keep, and so on. No one will know what Brandon Teena was thinking on New Year's Eve, 1993. Was he maybe telling himself that he would try sticking to one woman? That he would stop forging cheques and stealing money?

That day, in a farmhouse outside the town of Humboldt, Nebraska (population just over 5,000), Brandon, Philip De Vine, and Lisa Lambert, were shot and killed by two men. The men charged were the same two Brandon had accused of raping him on Christmas Eve six days before. Both of them had started out as Brandon's friends. John Lotter is now on death row. Thomas Nissen was granted immunity from the death sentence in exchange for testifying against Lotter.

At the time of the murders, Brandon was a young guy, only 21. He was not yet the most famous transgendered person in the world, not yet the subject of several books, including a novel, not yet the subject of a documentary *and* an Oscar-nominated movie, Hilary Swank not yet the actress who would win an Academy Award for playing him. If anything, Brandon was infamous with state police for a string of forged checks and other miscellaneous financial wrongdoings. The other segment of the population well acquainted with him were the girls in his hometown of Lincoln. According to the *New Yorker*'s John Gregory Dunne, Brandon was a "lady-killer of some proportion."[48]

When Brandon's real sex was revealed after his death, the first question everyone had was how were the women duped. Had they really been duped? The implicit question was whether these presumably small-town straight girls were in fact lesbians. And if not, how did they deal with Brandon, who like many female-to-male transsexuals is said to have not let his lovers touch him? Did they have sex? Sex in this instance being understood as requiring penetration, as if a woman would not, could not, be happy without it.

The other question in the rumors about Brandon's lovers was the same one that drove Nissen and Lotter to rape and kill Brandon: what's he got? What does this slim weakling got that within two months he's made his way through three women and gotten the local beauty to fall in love with him? What's he got that I don't?

So how did the women deal with Brandon's sex? Most have denied knowing Brandon was by birth a woman. To admit otherwise would leave them open to charges of lesbianism in a close-knit town. More hopefully, perhaps they also denied knowing Brandon's sex because to do so would be to rob him of the dignity of his identity. When Brandon made love to these women and when he courted them, he did so with all the graces and manners he would have thought necessary to land a girlfriend. The number of girlfriends and his petty cash crimes aside, with each woman he behaved like an old-fashioned gentleman. In return the women were at their best. *New York Times* writer and novelist Dinitia Smith imagines what may have gone through the girls' minds in her fictionalized account of the case, *The Illusionist.* "Best loyalty I could give Dean [Brandon] — call him what he wanted to be called. . . . Define him as he wanted to be defined," says one of Brandon's fictionalized girlfriends in Smith's book. "That was the most profound loyalty you could give someone."[49]

Ironically, the men who were convicted in Brandon's death now refer to him as a man. Having humiliated him in front of his girlfriend (in one incident trying to pull down his jeans and Jockeys to reveal he did not have a penis), having raped him, having proven who the real men are, they can now revert to how Brandon presented himself. Writing to Dunne about all the "what if's" that lead to the murders, Nissen persistently talks about Brandon as a he. This sentence is particularly startling, containing enough gradations of gender to satisfy a semantic pedant. "'What if, on Dec. 23 [the day of the rape] Brandon had told me, Tom, I'm really a girl and please take me home because I think I may get hurt. . . . He had the chance.'"

Had Brandon agreed to be a girl, he, Nissen would have reverted to his male role. He would have played the protector. Brandon's refusal to act like a girl led Nissen to force him to be a girl, to put him in her place. The questions the transgendered pose to our own sense of gender identity have never been clearer, and the challenge they pose to a two-gendered world rarely more harshly repelled.

Being transgendered has long been thought a pathology. To quote the full description in the *DSMA:* "Invariably there is the wish to live as a member of the other sex . . . People with the disorder usually complain that they are uncomfortable wearing the clothes of their assigned sex. . . . These people often find their genitals repugnant which may lead to persistent requests for sex reassignment by hormonal and surgical means . . . the estimated prevalence is one per 20,000 males and one per 100,000 for females." The World Health Organization also classifies gender dysphoria as a disorder. Mental explanations for the "condition" range from a physically and/or emotionally abusive childhood, to being encouraged to dress and act like the opposite gender at an early age.

Both explanations help to serve one purpose: that of protecting the single-gendered from questioning the two-gendered world and the security of their place in it. We will give the transgendered the right to vote and live among us but really we all know they belong in the kitchen. In the words of the transgendered activist and writer Kate Bornstein, "transsexuality is the only condition in Western culture for which the therapy is to lie."[50]

History is littered with evidence of the fate lying in wait for women who fail to lie successfully. Maria van Antwerpen, a Dutch woman of the 18th century, began living as a man when she was 27 and joined the army under the name Jan van Ant, 16-years-old. She was discovered over and over again. Each time she was punished. Each time she went back to wearing men's clothes. In August of 1748, Jan met the daughter of a sergeant and married her. After the marriage, Jan began working as a tailor, and his wife took in washing and looked after foster children. In three years of marriage, Jan's wife never discovered his true sex. In 1751, Jan was unveiled as Maria. His wife was laughed at and jeered in the streets. After another affair, Jan married again — this time a woman who knew about Maria but needed a husband because she was pregnant. When Jan was again discovered in 1765, he was sentenced to exile. At a point during judicial questioning in 1769 (when he was discovered for the third time) Jan was asked by the judges if she was a man or a woman. "By nature and character, a man, but in appearance, a woman," he responded. At the same trial, he also said what so many female-to-transsexuals have said and done since. That even when dressed in women's clothes, he wore men's garments underneath.[51] After his death in 1781, he was buried in a pauper's grave.

In 1934, Dorothy Lucille Tipton wrapped a sheet around her chest, pinned it tight with the help of a cousin, and became the saxophonist for a jazz band that allowed only men to join. Billy Tipton was born. Over the next 30 years, Tipton traveled on the road with various bands. In between, Tipton also had four wives, including one whom Diane Wood Middlebrook, Tipton's biographer, describes as resembling Sophia Loren. (What's he got?) His third wife, Maryanne Cattanach, said that the first time she danced with him, "he seemed to have a permanent hard-on." (Tipton wore his plaster prosthesis at all times.)

While his wives, like Brandon's girlfriends, said they did not know Tipton was a man, Billy played cat-and-mouse with his audiences. One joke went: Straight Man, "When did you first begin to like girls?" Billy: "When I found out they weren't boys." The deception was only discovered in 1989 by the coroner at Tipton's death. At 74, despite persistent pain, Tipton had refused to go to the doctor. He died of a bleeding ulcer rather than expose himself to the shame of having his female genitals discovered.[52]

In a two-gendered system, fitting into one or the other slot is crucial to being a part of society. Transsexuals are well aware of the denial of the established order that they represent: after all, one radical political activist group calls itself Transsexual Menace, or Transgender Menace. As well they should; they are a threat to any society that bases itself on fitting human complexity into boxes. And it's not just mainstream society that is unsure where and what kind of lines to draw. In 1991, the Michigan Women's Music Festival banned transsexuals from attending. Every August since a group of transsexuals calling themselves Son of Camp Trans set up booths outside the festival gates. And every August the festival re-affirms its policy: The event is "for womyn-born womyn, meaning people who were born and have lived their entire life experience as female."[53]

For a transgendered person to "pass" is to have access to a social (if not legal) identity, to a certain amount of respect from society, to the right to be called sir, or ma'am. Leslie Feinberg, an activist and transgendered man recalls that while she was transitioning into a he, people were often confused what to call her. "Here's your change, sir, I mean ma'am, I mean sir," they said. The more derogatory term, one that was appropriated by some f-to-m's later, was a he-she.

The he-she was a person in constant search for a world to call his own. Bars like San Francisco's Kelly's Alamo Club or New York's Sea Colony catered to working-class lesbian couples on Friday and Saturday nights. Living outside the heterosexual world, the couples still came up with their own rigid and ever-changing social code, one where butches courted femmes and stone butches would not allow any woman to touch them. In those pre-Stonewall days, police raids on the bars were frequent and merciless, the police throwing the butches in jail and raping them, while charging their femmes with prostitution when they found them soliciting on the street.[54] Butches could be thrown in jail for not wearing the mandatory three pieces of women's underwear, punishment not just for who they were sleeping with, but for transgressing their gender.

Meanwhile, decades before, safe in Hollywood where everything was allowed and encouraged as long as you were making money for someone, Marlene Dietrich's androgynous persona was seducing the world.

What fascinates me about these lives, that of Brandon, of Tipton, of Feinberg, is how they required constant self-examination and self-monitoring, how every gesture and word was not just what it was in itself but also a sign of the people creating themselves each time. Feinberg found that neither gender reflected who she was. After a double mastectomy and hormone treatments turned her into a man who could truly pass, Feinberg stopped taking hormones. Now, she lives in-between. Her picture on the back of various books show either a fine-featured man with blond hair wearing a natty suit or a reserved woman wearing no make-up. Take your pick.

Women and men must engage in a myriad of these convincing gestures every day to "pass." It is easy for me to say that to inhabit another gender would feel liberating. But to be a transsexual is not just to cross-dress and gender play, no Annie Lennox with a closely shaved carrot-top, or Madonna wearing a white tux. The transgendered are exiles from gender altogether. During an interview with writer Kate Bornstein, interviewer Shannon Bell suddenly exclaims, "I guess it's kind of a privilege to be able to play with gender."[55]

In *The Thief's Journal*, French writer Jean Genet chronicled another hidden world, similar to that of the lesbian bars of the fifties where gay men assumed roles depending on who their lovers were. It was a world made up of petty hustlers and their aristocratic protectors, sailors and former inmates; a world where desire did not just travel directly between a man and a woman, between the first and third drink with negotiations proceeding much as they have for millennia, but one where the rules and the roles can change and are open to the players to interpret. It was a world that as Jean-Paul Sartre said, was made up of constant choice,[56] where the only way to tell which option was right was to read the ever-shifting signs from the way a young man buckles his belt to the way he combs his hair. Such were the small acts of defiant self-creation that preserved and reinforced homosexual identity in a heterosexual society.

Like transgendered stories, these quests for identity are so compelling to me because they are infused with the desire and longing to create a whole self. It's not just that the whole world is a candy store that a he-she or she-he is not allowed into, it's also that they themselves are trapped in the store, their phantom double knocking on the door. The narrative of a transgendered transition is the classic story-telling quest, and all the more powerful because at its core is the quest for one's soul at its most intimate core. In comparison, single-gendered people seem a little, well, lacking in complexity.

Desire does not just live in private bedrooms but in the world, in every time we look at a couple crossing the street and even for a second, measure our love life against theirs; in every moment that we watch two people having sex on TV or in a movie and wonder why we never look as polished or as beautiful when we have sex; in every time we look at a picture of an attractive person and wonder if they would be interested in us, us in them; and so on. To say that desire is private is a lie.

So a transgendered person challenges not just our sense of identity, but also our understanding of desire. We desire men or women; would the tone of that desire change if it was for someone in between or would we simply fall in love?

The body is tough to beat. When women want to reaffirm their femaleness, a whole culture supports them. Large breasts courtesy of implants are socially sanctioned and celebrated. A very attractive woman I know once told me that if she had more money the first thing she would buy would be a pair of implants. I told her about the risks, told her she didn't need to do this. She was adamant. To me subjecting oneself to breast implants for cosmetic reasons seems an act of absolute insanity, a profound rejection of one's body and one's self and acceptance of the world's seeming verdict of you as defective. And yet this is what women dream of: more money to buy bigger breasts. Yet when a woman wants to have her breasts cut off because she wants to be a man, the treatment of her by hospitals afterwards can be dismissive and rudimentary. This is the cost of fighting against one's gender instead of reinforcing it.[57]

"One is not born a woman, but rather becomes one," wrote Simone de Beauvoir and a whole feminist revolution revolved around the sentence. One is not condemned to being lesser because of one's sex, but we can allow society to make it so. More radically, the sentence could also mean that one can be born a woman and become something else. Both interpretations see the self as ruler of the body and not the other way around. And yet any man who has measured his penis or any woman who has wondered whether her breasts are too small or too big would argue with that. The body is not, cannot, be irrelevant. For as long as we live among others, our bodies and our faces will be the first thing others see. We can resist, but can we truly conquer the carrying case? No wonder that living as something other than the genitals you were born with has been called an "act of everyday resistance."[58]

Cyber-space might seem to some to be the perfect testing ground for the relevance of bodies. Men pretending to be women is the most common occurrence in virtual reality: blondwench567 is really blondgeek567. One study found that 150,000 men had pretended to be women in chat rooms. Paradoxically, though blondwench567 may be a bearded guy swigging a beer and eating chips while moaning about how good a man's touch makes her feel, her body is of paramount importance. The chatter's whole identity is committed to the body he or she is impersonating. I once watched as a woman describing herself as a transsexual had cybersex with another woman in a chat room. Neither one of them ever stopped fetishizing the transsexual's body (real or imagined); their conversation was all about how the physical parts fit together. In the absence of real bodies and real sensations, the degree of description necessary to simulate a sex act in cyberspace makes the body central.

For much of the history of transgendered people, bodies have been stumbling blocks to becoming the other. The mastectomy scars, or the tiny incisions from implants; the under-developed constructed penis; or the not quite 100 per cent accurate vagina; the jaw line that was not quite soft enough to belong to a woman; the Adam's apple that was not quite pronounced enough to belong to a man. Some transsexuals modified their bodies not because they required physical proof of their identities but because society would not take them seriously otherwise. To gain legal rights transsexuals must prove they are of the gender with which they identify.

In two Ontario cases, female-to-male transsexuals were denied any spousal separation benefits simply because of their genitals. In one of the cases, the relationship had lasted for 25 years and was a legal marriage. The male partner of the couple had once been female, but had undergone a double mastectomy and a hysterectomy. The judge's ruling, however, relied entirely on the man's biological identity. "The genitalia of B . . . to my understanding, have in no way been touched surgically . . . ," the judge said. "A double mastectomy is not in itself an unusual event. Many females today undergo a hysterectomy. Indeed, I would anticipate we have many females who have had both surgical treatments, yet who continue completely as female."[59]

Confronted with an identity that could not be covered by existing laws, the judicial system was not elastic enough to account for the richness of human variety.

Under these circumstances, most people will attempt to cleave to the rules set by society. As Keith, one of the f-to-m's interviewed in Holly Devor's book, *FTM*, says, "the only reason for sex reassignment [is] that it was the only way for females to live their lives legitimately in those ways which society reserves for people who are deemed to be men.

"That's a society rule. In society we are forced to pick . . . some days I feel more feminine, some days I feel more masculine. . . . You've got to make up your mind and decide. . . . Actually, I've never been either. I really don't feel a part of either camp."[60]

As Keith suggests, in reality, many f-to-m's can't ever really join either camp: a woman can have a double mastectomy but to obtain a working penis is almost impossible. The being that is created is stranded in the land of the in-betweens.

Slowly, that state is becoming an alternative. "We were hesitant about giving hormones if people were not sure they wanted surgery, because you were promoting someone to the netherlands in between . . . [Now] we're becoming a little less concerned about someone surviving in the middle," said a psychiatrist at a Vancouver clinic in 1999.[61] The case of David Reimer, who was the subject of a gender experiment in which doctors turned him into a girl after a fire damaged his genitals would be unthinkable now. While Reimer's case has been used as evidence that you can't tinker with nature, his case also shows that as he himself has said, his body has not defined his identity. "These people," he said, talking about the psychiatrists who believed he may never fit into being a man, "gotta be pretty shallow if they think . . . the only reason why people get married and have children and have a productive life is because of what they have between their legs."[62]

As far back as the ancient Greeks, the person who lives in-between genders was privileged. The myth of Tiresias, who appears in Ovid's *Metamorphoses*, revolves around his being both man and woman. Born a man, Tiresias is turned into a woman for striking two snakes. Years later, he strikes them again and is turned into a man. When Zeus and Hera have an argument as to whether it's men or women who enjoy sex more, they bring in Tiresias, the only person who, having lived as both, knows the answer. "As far as love is concerned, the pleasure women experience is nine times more intense than that of men," he says. For this, Hera blinds him. As recompense, Zeus gave him the gift of prophecy. From then on, Tiresias's gift as a prophet has been linked to his sexual identity. As T.S. Eliot describes him in *The Waste Land*: "I Tiresias, though blind, throbbing between two lives, / Old man with wrinkled female breasts, can see."

For Native Indians, the transgendered are known as Two-Spirited people, or in the word used by colonizers to America "berdache." In northeastern Brazil in 1576, explorer Pedro de Magalhaes found women who dressed like men, went to war, and hunted with the men. According to Jesuit Jacques Marquette, the two-spirited people were "summoned to the Councils, and nothing [was] decided without their advice. Finally, through their profession of leading an Extraordinary life, they pass for . . . Spirits — or persons of consequence."[63] As was the case 100 years later, mainstream society was bent on straightening out the genders. United States federal agents in the 1890s are said to have entered Crow reservations and forced the bade (the modern equivalent of the m-to-f) to cut off their long hair and wear men's clothing.

What would a world where two-spirited people are accepted look like? By the end of the 1994 movie *The Crying Game*, Stephen Rea has come to accept the bifurcated identity of Dil, the same m-to-f he so famously ran away from at the beginning of the film. The film, which has unrolled like an *English Patient* on speed, ends with Dil visiting Rea in prison. "Honey, how are you?" says Dil. "Don't call me that," says Rea, wincing, but also leaving little doubt who he'll make his life with once he is released.

Della Grace (now Del LaGrace Volcano), has shot women transitioning to men. Her photographs, of a growing constructed penis, of mastectomy scars, show the changing physical body both as a work-in-progress and as a thing in itself, the physical expression of a third sex.[64] Instead of making the body into something acceptable to the viewer, it too becomes an outlaw, outside conventional notions of beauty and grace. In Grace's photos, the body is an open, rhetorical question: what kind of behaviors, what kind of emotions go with this body? How does this body cry and how does it hurt and how does it love? What separates Grace's bodies from older photographs of transsexuals, those in which men transformed themselves into exact replicas of women, or women (à la Greta Garbo in *Morocco*) into men, is that they do not conform. When I look at the bodies in Grace's photographs, my first instinct is to compare them with my own and then by association with the photographs of images of other women, other men, that we all carry around in our minds. They are something else altogether, something that used to be female and is now male but not really.

It's that "not really" that challenges and threatens. It's also that "not really" that has the power to free us from the prison of gender. To decide that identity is inextricably tied to biology is not just to decide that I am a woman because I have the physical characteristics of one, but also to decide that as a woman I must behave in certain ways. Playing with gender — dressing as a man, undressing as a woman — might help me to not feel so constrained, but it also only goes so far. After all, my toys are still taken from a chest of toys in which each toy has a certain, fixed meaning.

"Gender is a cult," says Bornstein. "Membership in gender is not based on informed consent. There is no way out without being ridiculed and harassed."[65] The rules being challenged by the transgender movement are about the exchange of power underlying any relationship, but especially about the society-sanctioned exchange of power that wants to rule all our interactions. That says men take out the garbage and women do what? Dust? Consent to being fucked? As opposed to fucking? From the glass ceiling, to catcalls on the shop floor; to realizing far, far, far too late that if only you'd played the good girl and not called, not kissed first, not fucked in the middle of the afternoon because you just bloody wanted to, you would have gotten some respect; that if only you'd played the bad boy and hadn't returned her phone calls, she'd be chasing you; to realizing that your female boss is as enmeshed in the gender system as the boys; to thinking about how everyone blames each other and men never do anything, and they are after one thing and one thing only and it's women's job to keep them from getting it; and women just want to marry a rich guy and sit on their ass eating bon-bons; and men can't allow themselves the pleasure of being coveted but they can covet their daughter's best friend because she's young and pretty and knows no better . . .

Are we really so committed to this vision of ugliness?

The night before I finished this chapter, attempting to grapple with why I had become so fascinated with female-to-male transsexuals, I had a dream. In the dream, I was at a funeral parlor with the small, little girl-voiced woman from *Poltergeist.* Pointing to the jars of ashes lining the walls, I asked her, "Is this it? This is what comes of us?" She nodded, then said, "Yeah, but you come back in two days." "Just two days?" I asked her. "Yeah, as someone else." "Do you know who you were before?" "No, never."

I thought about this for a while then also thought that perhaps that's why children often seem so precocious at certain moments. Because they have been someone else and someone else before that and until they become adults, their old personalities are still there. (It was a dream.) I told her this.

"Something of the other is always there, yes. In some people," she agreed. Then I woke up. It could have meant anything and it meant a lot of things at that particular point in my life. But it could also have meant that like women who have become men, or like men who have become women, we all have something of the other in us. I hope we do anyway.

CHAPTER **SEVEN**

CANDY54 SEEKS BOYTOY67

The images are slow to appear on my computer screen. Disjointed, broken, every once in a while a square bit of the picture comes in fuzzy, sharp edges bit-mapped in many colors. I'm watching an X-rated video from the comfort of my study. I should be working, but the Net is a wonderful tool for procrastinators.

I didn't have to put on a pair of sunglasses and a broad-rimmed hat, pull the collar of my trench coat up to my neck and quietly slip into an adult video store to take my place among the other furtive customers. I didn't even have to leave the house. A few clicks of my mouse and I had free access to one of hundreds of adult sites on the Internet. You can pay for this — if you're foolish. Smart adult customers get their fix by consulting the constantly updated lists of so-called "hacked" passwords posted on sites built just for this purpose. A mix of illegally obtained verification and temporary ID provided by adult sites to generate paying customers, these password sites started up as soon as pictures of naked people sprouted on the Net.

In a cyber world where nothing is forbidden anymore, these sites persist in the quaint notion that by going to them and getting into pay sites for free you are partaking of forbidden fruit. However far the seamy side of the Net has come, the hunt for hard-to-obtain passwords has remained unchanged. Functioning like a private club of ironic porn connoisseurs, the sites not only provide the fake identification you need to bulldoze your way into the smooth pages of the high-priced Sizzle.com, Playboy.com, Hustler.com, or Cybererotica.-com, among many other smaller, short-lived sites, but also an informal rating system. Anyone can mail in a password and a rating; or even just a review of the site. As the Internet sex industry has developed, the password sites have started to issue warnings. "This site is sick. . . . Try it only if you have a strong stomach. . . . Whoever came up with this site is a pervert. . . . Warning: the girls here look really young."

It's in these warnings that I find the spectacle of sex on the Net at its most absurd. Here are a bunch of hackers, maybe pimply teenagers, maybe dot.com serfs with pot of gold dreams, maybe just computer techies with a couple of free hours on their hands and nothing better to do than review sex sites. This group of misfits is our last bastion of the sex police. Exposed every day to increasingly more bizarre depictions of sex, they are right up to date on what is acceptable adult content. In comparison to the rough measure of a child filter which blocks all adult sites, password hackers are discerning border guards. This month horses and women are acceptable, last month they would have come with a strong warning.

The frontier of Net sex is moving ever further. Much hand wringing attends it. If I were to believe the newspapers and magazines and television, sex on the Net should alarm us. The Lumiere brothers caused a stampede in 1896 when the Parisians seated in a café thought the train coming at them on screen was a real locomotive behind the screen. Screaming, they ran outside afraid they would be run over. The Internet porn industry is causing a similar stampede in psychology circles. Unions crumble in the face of the husband's (it's rarely the wife's) addiction to anonymous sexual images, workers are fired for sneaking a peek at fake videos of Cameron Diaz and Michelle Pfeiffer "covered in cum," teenagers' mores and behaviors are irreparably damaged by hours spent gazing at nude pictures of 18- and 19-year-olds. Even sex crimes can be aided and abetted by anonymous chat rooms, where the mythical pedophile or rapist stalks his prey behind the security of an assumed and unthreatening personality. According to Minneapolis sex addiction therapist Elizabeth Griffin, co-author of *In the Shadow of the Net: Breaking Free of Compulsive Online Sexual Behavior*, porn is "the crack cocaine of the Internet world."

Last year, writer Garrison Keillor was besieged with e-mail from readers of his advice column, Mr. Blue, on *Salon*. Keillor, a Midwesterner gifted with a sense of proportion and a sensibility that is alarmed by very little in the spectrum of human behavior, had advised a young woman to stop snooping on her father as he downloaded dirty pictures. The women in the family thought his habit was disgusting and had taken it upon themselves to barge in on him. The letters were outraged. Pornography on the Net is destroying marriages, the letter writers fumed. Keillor relented slightly, but held his ground. A man needs his space.

Who is right? Perhaps there is a bit of reality in some of the "my-husband-has-been-possessed-by-dirty-pictures" scenarios. Whether it's enough to justify the up to $1000 counseling sessions the sex addict therapists sometimes charge is something only someone looking at divorce papers can answer. To the Pandora's box of troubles that can afflict any individual, we can add the lure of Internet sex. The alarm hides the more painful and also hopeful truth about sex on the Net — most of the people who use it are simply other human beings looking for someone to keep them company. Net sex is the cyberworld at its most nakedly paradoxical. A network that isolates us into individual users and consumers, our most focused relationship with the computer in front of us, it also has the ability to make us intimates of people on the other side of the globe. You can't leap out of a real bed if things are going badly without provoking a crisis, but you can claim a technical problem crashed your system. Still, leaping into the virtual bed is rarely just an exploration trip, it's an attempt to find someone to talk to and care about, however briefly. Naïve? I don't think so.

For me, the question of how did we get to the point where we are debating the merits, or perils, of cyber-relating is not an abstract issue. The same Wild West impulse that seems to motivate sex hackers —

to make the untamed frontier of Net sex their own — has been responsible for my own trips into the world of Net sex for years. As cyber guru Julian Dibbell put it in an article explaining how it happened that he found his personal erotic nirvana in gazing upon sexual photos of pregnant women, I found that sometimes trolling for Net porn can reduce anxiety. "I don't claim it's the healthiest approach. But it does calm the nerves, at least for a little while,"[66] Dibbell writes and I can only concur. One day I would like to sit down with him and attempt to figure out exactly what it is about watching the number of bytes downloading a dirty picture or movie into our machines that soothes the daily fray.

In any case, there you have it, courtesy of this most modern and unexpected form of Zen meditation. I was there when cyber-sex happened in "moos," where you had to use Unix-style commands to indicate your actions; there when cyber-sex advanced to the next stage and whole chat rooms become devoted to the topic of extramarital affairs and cheap air deals that would fly you out to meet the woman or man of your techno-assisted dreams; there when dirty pictures were only found in ftp directories built by horny computer students at Texas A&M University; there when the first sex for sale sites started sprouting up; and there when live sex shows were still a novelty.

Like a tourist who can still recall the glory of Acapulco in the fifties, I yearn for those years when free porn on the Net was difficult to find and the paying kind ridiculously expensive to contemplate and the mere idea of sites devoted to underage models or extreme sex pictures would inspire trepidation in the hearts of law-fearing adult site entrepreneurs. It only took a few years for the adult sex industry to blossom on the Net and for every piece of primo terrain to be landscaped with ever more garish and specialized offers. Few want to admit it, but it was the Net porn industry that led the way in technological innovation. First to use streaming media, first to use streaming audio, first to widely adopt the use of revenue-generating click-through banner ads, the e-commerce pyramid scheme where everyone posting a banner from another site earns a couple of cents when you, the customer, clicks on the ad.

In 1997, porn star Danni Ashe told the *Wall Street Journal* she was raking in $2-million a year in profits with her site, Danni's Hard Drive. At the time it was a fairly basic photo gallery with the option to buy videos. That sum has vastly increased. Estimates put the overall number of Web sites that sell sex in some form at 100,000 and rising. Revenue is projected to hit over $1-billion this year. The industry would like that sum to increase to at least $20-billion. After all, the other sin businesses, like tobacco or gambling, total annual profits of about $50-billion. The television revolution built nations of couch potatoes, sex sites on the Net hope to build nations of home office sex addicts. (The hidden dangers of telecommuting.) Seminars at a recent industry expo for the Net sex business promised to teach entrepreneurs with a sexy twinkle in their eye how to get their share of the future: "A Studio in Every Home: The Impact of the Coming Broadband Revolution," was one seminar title.

My own home studio, if a few hours here and there can be called that, has long been closed. Every once in a while, I take a look around: check that the old stand-bys are still there and wonder at the luck that made people prescient enough to get in on the ground floor back in oh, the stone of age of 1995? Why, oh why, did I not think to register the site www.sex.com? I knew that if anything is going to sell on the Net, sex will be it. But no, it had to be some clever chap, now millions richer.

The business side of the industry fascinates me today. But the thrill of going where I was not supposed to, a thrill that most resembled the feeling I had when as a 14-year-old I found a hardcover copy of *Delta of Venus* on my parents' bookshelf and proceeded to peruse it on a weekly basis, is long gone. When I look at images that used to turn me on, they have no evocative power over me anymore. If Alice had come out the other side of the Wonderland rabbit hole, I think she'd feel much as I do about the world of sex on the Net. Bored, jaded, dismissive, and maybe just a little bit sad.

I'm lying in bed late at night in the middle of fall, as usual unable to sleep. A picture is forming in my mind of a guy I've been corresponding with by e-mail for almost a month now. I'll call him Stephen — since I don't know any Stephens. We send each other two page letters about our day, sometimes at the beginning of the day, sometimes at night, sometimes both. From what I know about him, he might be a good match for me. If he were a personal ad, you could describe him as creative, kooky, well-read, artistic — he also claims he's cute. On paper, his life might even seem exciting: he works for a new media company. After work, though, his major source of entertainment seems to be going to buy obscure CDs by European dance bands. Eventually, he makes his way home to an apartment he describes as too small. He has a few friends, he says, but in the month I've known him he is more often than not at home watching television, playing video games, listening to music, or reading. On Saturday nights, he does his laundry.

What is perplexing me is that he has not yet asked for my phone number, or suggested we have coffee. I don't particularly like having a pen pal across town; someone who knows what I do for a living, a good idea of where I live and my first name, but I don't know what he looks like. Everything I know about him could be a lie. There's also the problem of spending as much as an hour engrossed in writing and reading e-mails to someone I may never meet.

Dating could be frustrating and precarious in the pre-Internet days; now another layer of complication has been added. So why have I started up a sputtering e-mail romance with someone I have never met? Partly, it was an accident. I had read an article in the *New York Times* about a writer who wanted to see how he would fare if he did not leave his house for a month and lived solely through the Internet. He conducted his social life on a Net matchmaking site. Single at the time and having had no luck meeting someone through the conventional — let's go on a date and see if we can stand each other — methods, I wanted to try something new. I surfed on over to where the *New York Times* guy had found a temporary e-mail pen pal, filled out a remarkably honest profile of myself and sat back to see what would happen. Within a few days, I had five or six e-mail letters from men describing themselves. The guy I was corresponding with was the only one to whom I responded.

The site I had signed up on had an interesting understanding of the dating game. It allowed members to track when their e-mails had been opened by the recipient, how many e-mails the recipient had sent, and how many of those were to the member doing the cyber stalking. In other words, while you might not know whether in real life your imaginary friend was twenty years older than he claimed, whether he was married with a large brood of children, or really a single, urban, wanna-be loft dweller, you could track if he was dating someone else in cyberspace. Even that was not full proof. He or she could, after all, have many other identities on the same site. I, for example, had two: the me that was writing to this man, and the me that was a much wilder, sexually curious, and very much liberated version and was a research experiment for this book. My second identity, however, received no mail. Apparently, the other people on the site were seeking a potential partner for a relationship. Like a paranoid girlfriend who checks her partner's phone messages after surreptitiously gaining access to his phone password, I was checking Stephen's page for the number of e-mails he was sending out. Far as I could tell, he was only writing to me. With letters flying back and forth, the poor guy probably didn't have time for anyone else.

I was reaching the point where I wanted to meet and see if it was worthwhile continuing. I had consulted on-line sites devoted solely to the etiquette of Net dating. All the friendly advice ladies who had dubbed themselves overnight experts on the topic had the same words of wisdom: meet early and in person.

The next morning, I suggested as much by asking how long he thought was reasonable to wait before having a coffee. In response, he invoked the same caution a flesh-and-blood man may invoke when he feels things are "going too fast." Best to enjoy things without any pressure. But if I was feeling uncomfortable, I was not bound to write to him anymore, he added. After that, we exchanged a couple more e-mails. Then I simply stopped. He never wrote to ask why or offer a meeting. For both of us, I think, something was not quite clicking. And yet somewhere in this city there resides a man I have never met or seen but I could tell you the details of his relationship with his family, his likes and dislikes, what he eats for dinner, when he wakes up and goes to bed, and the problems he has with his friends. He could tell you some of the same things about me. And the big question? No, we never had cyber-sex. Neither one of us brought it up, it's not why we were writing.

We were writing because in the absence of a real person who would listen to how our day went and at least in my case, wariness about real-life relationships, this was the best we could come up with. Nothing came of it, but for a month in an otherwise ho-hum, sometimes lonely fall, writing to Stephen made life more interesting. It was a secret I carried with me when I got on buses and streetcars looking for someone who resembled how he described himself.

I stopped going to the site the same day I stopped writing to him. I don't know how many more e-mails he sent to other women, or if he continued to search for someone in his town on a site with headquarters hundreds of miles away in another country. I've never been curious, the way I am curious about the whereabouts and romantic lives of former boyfriends. But I like to think that he no longer lives in an apartment he feels is too small and that he no longer comes home by himself every night; even perhaps that another woman was a better match and she was more patient and they met and are living happily ever after.

Stephen is not the only person I've met through the Net. What is remarkable is to what extent I remember the people I talked to as well as if I had met them in person. A few years before Stephen, during another "dry spell," I briefly frequented chat rooms. I had no patience for the idle chitchat that passes for conversation; what I wanted to know is what cybersex, what everybody was talking about at the time, would be like. I had chatted in multi-user created environments, otherwise known as "moos" when they first appeared. More like a virtual game of Dungeons and Dragons, moos allowed members to build their own rooms and create private environments where they could talk to only those they invited in. The issues that arose then in the cyberworld are the same ones that exist now. Insulting other users (flaming), harassing them by pestering them with public or private messages, or even, in one early case in which a woman accused a man of cyber-raping her, assuming another's identity.

For the technology pioneers who believed that the Net held the potential for global communication free of discrimination, where we could all be, and be judged, by our own best, unguarded selves, these actions were a sore disappointment. As chat rooms developed, that initial idealism receded even further. The rude and inarticulate chatter of late-night chat rooms crowded with supposed buxom blondes from Texas and former football players from Arizona has little in common with the social and political debates that happened on the early days of San Francisco's The Well community. And yet.

The day when I first tried out cyber-sex I logged onto a primitive sex chat room. The text was simply white letters on a black background, but you could easily send private messages to another user. A couple of hours later, after establishing that both of us had a liking for the original French version of *La Femme Nikita*, I had gotten to know the sexual peccadilloes of a British man who claimed to be stuck at work late in London. Across a five-hour time zone and an ocean, I had engaged in a pretty intimate act with a complete stranger. In between describing what we were doing, Harry cracked jokes. He did not claim to have a huge member, he did not claim to be particularly good-looking, he did not claim anything about himself that would show him to be anything more than a fairly regular English chap. Like a real-life lover, he had his techniques, rhythm, and interests and diversions. He was quite fun and if I had lived in London I would have hoped to be able to meet him. Probably it would not have worked out. We accidentally met in the same room months later and while we remembered each other instantly and tried to start up where we had left off, this time there was no magic. The things we had imagined and which by the nature of their novelty had delighted us both, had already become old and tired. Without the sense of touch and smell, our individual likes and dislikes were separate from the bodies and personalities in which they were housed. We had nothing to connect about; like a pair who go on to date after a one-night stand, the instant intimacy did not give us access to the more patient task of unraveling our selves for the other's pleasure.

The second time I tried cyber-sex cured me of it. In between Harry and, I'll call him Ed, there had been several abortive attempts at seeing how other men act in the cyber bed. Overall, Americans were the absolute worst, jumping from "What do you look like?" to the end of the story in a flat five-minutes. All that was required on my end was to type in "oh, that's great" a few times and they seemed to be quite content. No humor and no finesse. I never met a Frenchman on the Net; the Spaniards' seductions did not translate well in the virtual realm sounding more like a Julio Iglesias song; Italians were annoyingly coy. I stayed away from the Canadians because they might inadvertently live around the corner from me. Overall, I would have to recommend the Brits; for creativity and the fewest spelling mistakes, those in the S/M lifestyle. In real life, I lack the experience to give the same range of ratings.

Cyber-sex gave me a taste of experiences that I did not have in real-life, allowed me to explore what it would have been like to be a different person without ever having to put myself on the line, or live with any consequences. In a time of short-lived, unstable relationships, AIDS, and ever-present hysteria about Internet-related crimes, sex with a stranger you will truly never see again was for me the equivalent of the best conversations with travelers on a train. We invaded each other's lives but left no tracks.

Ed was an American. He lived in San Francisco and said he was about 15 pounds over the weight he wanted to be. We talked about the city for a while and how you can hitch a ride on the back of the streetcars without paying for the ride and about the crab sandwiches with butter and mayonnaise on warm buns you can get in Monterey for $5 bucks. Ed was also about ten years older than me and he had a relaxed way of writing. I imagined that he would talk slowly and liked to drink wine and read in bed. We were engaged in other activities for about three hours. If in real life, sex might take an hour when both parties are well rested and have time to spare, everything is made longer on-line. Those who think that women like foreplay and afterglow as much as the act itself may be surprised to hear that even a woman has her limits. Three hours is just more time than I have. I liked Ed, though.

The Internet introduces a false sense of intimacy. Unlike a train trip where the decision to meet again might be fraught with complications, the decision to meet again on the Net requires only another commitment of a couple of hours. Repeat the experience a few times, however, and you may find yourself at the office of a travel agent. I was completely uninterested in this latter possibility. The risks seemed outrageously high, the potential of a relationship with someone in another country very low. And anyway, what would I say to the children? I met your Daddy on the Net? We cyber-ed and I knew right away he was the one? No, I want to leave these experiences to the generation after me. Also, I most certainly did not want to have what has since become a common ceremony: the cyber-wedding. Nor did I want to find myself with my cyber-procured beau chatting to the room where I had met him while he glanced over my shoulder, as I watched one couple do one evening.

Ed wanted to meet again. In the post-cyber glow, I agreed. I thought about it for a while. When the appointed day and time came, I didn't even log on to the site where we were to meet. Perhaps he made such assignations all the time, several a day with different women. I hoped he did. There had been a note of real yearning in his messages to me (one which quite likely would not have been there if mine were not similar in return). Most likely, we were both having a bad spell of the other gender, but this was no solution.

I cannot bring myself to apply sexual terms to entanglements on the Web. Much of sex might be in the mind, but not so much of it as to make the body irrelevant in deciding whether or not actual physical acts have taken place. I do think having a cyber-relationship with someone while with a real-life partner is an emotional betrayal, but different in kind than a physical betrayal. In many ways, the emotional and intellectual energy required to have a continuing affair with a cyber partner far exceeds that of a one-evening assignation with a stranger met at a party or in a bar. Part of the reason I stopped responding to Stephen's e-mails is because our interaction demanded the same degree of responsiveness of me as a real partner would, without the majority of the benefits. My encounters were experimental and comforting in their own anonymous fashion.

Years later, all I remember are the personalities of the people, not what we typed into our computers. These affairs, if the term can be charitably stretched to include such short-term unreal dalliances, exist in a remote corner of my mind, one apparently stripped of the sentimental power of real memories. I simply smile to think of the people I have never met and never will recognize, so far away, and yet of whom I could spill indiscreet secrets. And they of me.

For some, life on the Net spills over into the real world. At a party, late in the evening, when most of the other guests had gone home, and the stragglers had turned into early-morning guests, the subject of who had cyber-ed came up. While some of us fessed up that we had typed dirty words to people in far away countries, one acquaintance told a story of repeated encounters with people she had met in chat rooms on the Web. At one point, she had traveled for over a day to visit someone she'd had late-night conversations with over the phone while his wife was sleeping in their bedroom. The visit to him was the fourth time she had met in person with a chat/phone pal. Others had come to visit her, she said, but invariably, after meeting them, the mystery and excitement paled in the face of the obstacles to a long-term union. Quite simply, they did not know each other and would have almost no opportunity to get to know each other and plenty for misunderstandings.

Roger was different. It had been six months from the time they first chatted to when she visited him. She recalled how long it took to learn to expect the ringing of the phone in the middle of the night after his wife was asleep. He was, of course, unhappy in his marriage. Laughing, she explained that the visit turned out to be a disaster. The town he had described as small was really a bland suburb with only a pizza joint, a gun shop with a practice area for target shooting, and a Blockbuster video for entertainment. His apartment bore the imprint of his wife — away on a business trip — with her earrings, lingerie, clothing, Visa bills, and soaps and potions in the bathroom.

The strangeness of the situation set in after she had been using the wife's night cream for the fourth night in a row. The virtual space they had created in their mind turned real, but its physical attributes seemed as imaginary as if they were still describing a physical environment on screen. "It was like being in a bunker," she told us. On the fifth night, the schism between her body and her mind threatened to lead to a nervous breakdown. She went to the airport and waited for a stand-by flight. She hasn't logged on to any chat rooms since, but almost a year later received an e-mail from her former paramour telling her of his divorce and his new girlfriend, another woman he had been talking to in the same room where they had originally met.

There was a variety of reactions, dulled as they were by the time and our inebriated and sleepy condition. The issue of adultery, the main topic that the mainstream media trumpets when it runs articles on the threat of Internet sex, was not even brought up. If it hadn't been her, it would have been someone in town. Only the distance made the enormity of their actions seem more severe, more calculated. Eventually, someone at the party spoke up.

"Why didn't you look for someone here?" she was asked. By now, the woman who had told the story did have a boyfriend who lived in the same city. At the time, though, she "didn't know." While we were surprised at her story, a whole industry has sprung up which takes Internet sex for granted. Even the *Complete Idiot's Guide* line of books, which started out years ago with the *Complete Idiot's Guide to DOS*, now includes a guide to on-line dating and another for on-line sex. *Internet Soul Mates* holds out the promise of finding the love of your life on-line. And a series of books for teens follows the love travails of the workers at @cafe, the "hippest coffee in San Francisco . . . [with] the coolest Internet site."

Contrast this image of effortless and antiseptic success with what relationships in real life sometimes end up looking like. Somewhere in one of Charles Saatchi's mansions, a room is devoted to Tracey Emin's bed project. An unmade bed, surrounded by soiled underwear, used condoms, empty alcohol bottles, ashtrays resting precariously on its duvet, the art installation caused a roar of outrage when it was shown as part of Britain's annual Turner exhibit in 1999. But the unapologetically titled *My Bed* is one of the most accurate depictions of the messiness of psyches in the real world. In virtual reality, you can have sex without anyone looking inside your bedroom.

If for a select few, cyber relationships changed their lives, for most of us the possibility of meeting people on-line will not change anything. At least not as long as the vast majority of the world's population is far from having the economic or technological resources to spend great amounts of time on-line. The people we are chatting to, be they in Australia, France, Italy, Chile, or California, are more like us than even some of our next-door neighbors. In this world, an online friend is just a twist on the long-distance relationship.

Not so long ago, I was talking to a chatting "newbie," someone who has just discovered the world of chat rooms and instant connections. He was fresh, with at least a few weeks to go before the weariness set in. "I'm really good at this," he explained. What he is good at is keeping strangers interested in talking to him. Watching his words form on screen, he admires his own creativity and the way the response he was hoping for materializes. Before scoring his first e-mail address, he studied the behavior of other men by posing as a young woman. "They were just 'what do you look like? Do you want to sit on my face?'

"I pick someone with an interesting name and then I ask them if they're an artist," he explained.

His aims? (Before someone shudders that this is exactly the kind of predatory man women on-line shy away from.) He simply likes flirting with women far away, bridging the distance between continents with a few well-placed compliments. And genuine human curiosity. Sexual attraction has always been the lubricant to love, the Internet prolongs the hormone-high of the infatuation stage. You won't find love on-line, but you can fall in love every day.

CHAPTER **EIGHT**

WHERE DID YOU GET THAT WHIP?

"I could give you my personal definition of love. Or I could at least tell you what it makes me think of. Not roses, bells, hearts, even broken ones. I think of a thin, round, black leather case which was lying at the bottom of my wardrobe with the shoes. . . . Snug in the leather, curved together one on another, a nicely heavy metaphor for many things, but to me they mean only love.
"Ever tried them? Handcuffs?"

— A.L. Kennedy.[67]

I get to know Victoria and Alana after I call the number in their ad at the back of a weekly Toronto entertainment paper. The first time I call, they tell me that they have been talking about writing a book. I try and flatter them by saying something like "Those who can't do, write." Victoria laughs.

Actually Victoria doesn't laugh much and when she does she does so quietly, in a voice that sounds as if it was ordained to be that of an S/M mistress. As it turns out, she is the submissive one. Alana is the dominatrix. At 28, she's several years younger than Vic, and she says she started doing this stuff after being a sub for many years. Her first relationship was with an older man, he was 30 when she was 15, and he made her do all sorts of things she didn't want to. After another relationship went much the same way she decided she wanted to be treated better, that she deserved to be treated better.

On the phone, she gleefully tells me about a man who had come to see them that afternoon. He wanted a golden shower and he wanted to clean their kitchen floor. They obliged him in the first and let him do the second. While he was taking a shower, Alana says, they checked to see if he had money. He didn't. They found his wallet and therefore his real name and threatened to call his wife. In his wallet, they also found his brother's business card. The brother was a lawyer. Later they will tell me that he was also a member of the Jewish community and had they blown the whistle on him he could have really suffered.

We make an appointment to talk in person a week or so later. What ends up happening is by no means the definitive look into the S/M community, or into the psychology of the men who are attracted to the duo's services, or into the women who provide those services. For that, you would need to spend months, if not years, living 24/7 in the lifestyle. Or perhaps like Toni, a New York dominatrix interviewed by *Village Voice* journalists Howard Smith and Cathy Cox, start out at 17 after picking up from your mom.[68]

What my experience with them does give me is the revelation that no fantasy is as powerful as the one that is not satisfied, no world so weak in its grasp on the imagination as the one that is experienced. That the fuss that has been made over S/M — by early feminist writers opposed to it as well as by those who find psychological fulfillment in its embrace — is far more exciting than the reality. Does S/M tell us anything about ourselves, except that sometimes we want a little (or a lot) of power and dominance with our sex, that not every night has to start and end with a cuddle? I don't think so. It tells us nothing except what we have always known: human sexuality is a multi-layered thing and what turns me on may not turn you on. Or vice-versa.

So why has so much been made of S/M lately? Why are nights devoted to leather fetish parties at clubs always packed with hundreds of people donning costumes? Could it be simply because as much as S/M is becoming accepted into the mainstream — in an episode of the vanilla TV series *Party of Five*, a couple on their honeymoon engaged in silk scarf bondage — it still has the lure of the forbidden and of the possibility of reinventing our selves? As long as society is committed to the monogamous couple in a long-term union, anything that toys with that conception will turn our crank in unexpected ways. The feminist Sheila Jeffreys may argue that "heterosexual sex is an S/M romance," but that's giving it a degree of excitement that a late night quickie does not possess. For however short a time, S/M holds out the promise that we are as bad as Josey Wales, and that we will be punished for it.

What's really remarkable is not that this has an allure, but that the allure has been so thoroughly analyzed, dissected, and most often, found deviant. Once upon a time, what someone did in the privacy of their bed was simply what someone did in the privacy of their bed. As long as they were not hurting anyone, or no one complained, they could proceed. In the 19th century, however, as the French historian and philosopher Michel Foucault argues, sexual behavior came under the scientific microscope. A man who committed sodomy with another man was no longer just engaging in the act, he became defined as a member of the species "homosexual". The Marquis de Sade was condemned for his violent sexual practices, but it was only a century later that his predilections became known as sado-masochistic.

As always Freud is to blame. He classified fantasies involving sadomasochism as a pathology and speculated that they were related to witnessing children being beaten. Seeing their peers hit made children aware of adults' superior strength. As adults, even though some of their sexual development was "normal," fantasies of children being subjugated to the will of their elders ruled his S/M patients' sexual imagination. Sadism was connected for Freud to infantile sexual development, which in adults progresses to sexuality centered in the genitals; masochism was sadism turned in against itself out of guilt. Regardless of the specifics, Freud indicted all his patients: "My male cases . . . comprised only a few who did not exhibit some other gross injury to their sexual activities; again they included a fairly large number of persons who would have to be described as true masochists in the sense of being sexual perverts."[69]

Churches might not be thrilled, but some of their members could have well served as Freud's test cases. Religious flagellation, argued the psychiatrist Havelock Ellis, was known to have an erotic side effect and penalties were inflicted on priests who sought to derive pleasure from administering the flogging. "The Inquisition," Ellis wrote, "was accustomed to prosecute the priest who, in prescribing flagellation as a penance, exerted it personally, or caused it to be inflicted on the stripped penitent in his presence, or made a woman penitent discipline him."[70] Good to know they had some standards.

You don't have to look to the Inquisition to see S/M condemned. In recent history, feminism has told women that the only way to liberate themselves is by giving up their old submissive roles. And so it is hardly surprising if feminists of the seventies vocally denounced S/M as just another way for the patriarchy to literally force women right back into the missionary position, at least in the bedroom. But listening to the words of some of the historians of S/M could make even a contrarian feminist start to think about whether the practice might be good for women. After all, women are often tops during S/M, making what some say to be man's essential weakness visible at last. "In the sexual demands of man's nature will be found the motives of his weakness towards woman. He is enslaved by her, and becomes more and more dependent upon her as he grows weaker, and the more he yields to sensuality,"[71] wrote Krafft-Ebbing, the author of *Psychopathia Sexualis*, the Bible of perversities. It is this sensual devotion that author Thomas Murray identifies as the dominatrixes' siren call. The "entire concept of female domination seems to have its roots in courtly love, in which the emphasis — though supposedly platonic — was actually on the woman controlling both the tenor of the relationship and the behavior of the man who was her servant in love."[72] In other words, Guinevere could have gotten herself a business card and a closet full of toys and gone into business as Lady Guinevere, with Lancelot as her slave.

S/M has penetrated into the straight mainstream after a lengthy incubation in the homosexual world. The lesbian writer Pat Califia was writing about finding both sensual pleasure and therapeutic release in S/M back in the early eighties. The San Francisco S/M lesbian mag, *On Our Backs* and the city's lesbian S/M collective, Chamois, opened up the subject for discussion within the lesbian community. The words "top" and "bottom" were first used by gay men. Now everyone talks about being a top or a bottom, and few don't know that consent in S/M "play" is indicated by the words green, yellow, and red. No wonder I don't find it thrilling. Traffic lights are traffic lights are traffic lights; spontaneity is their fatal flaw.

In my more irreverent moments, I've even wondered if perhaps those in the S/M lifestyle full-time do it because it's trendy. De Sade's writing can be bought anywhere now, in fancy, beautifully designed trade paperback editions that look stylish on any IKEA bookshelf. Seeing him portrayed as a freedom of speech fighter by Geoffrey Rush in *Quills,* it's easy to forget that the Marquis first got in trouble for pouring sealing wax into the lash wounds he had inflicted on a prostitute. Somehow, his rich wife was oblivious, allowing him to run through her cash to procure an ever-growing selection of girls to satisfy his urges. By the time he emerged from prison for a time at the age of 50 he was so obese he could hardly walk. (But never mind. A 30-year-old actress tended to his needs.)

His life of excess would suggest that there was definitely something wrong with the Marquis. Part of me thinks that even people who seek consent before inflicting pain do have something wrong with them. The wrong usually, though, is simply that they have been hurt in some way. As Juliette, a professional dominatrix in New York who came by her trade after some years spent as a prostitute explains, she liked her job partly because it constituted revenge. "By this time I was pretty hardened and I enjoyed beating and humiliating men who had done the same to me. . . . I hated all of these bastards."[73]

From this, it's not a huge leap to argue that practising S/M is in some way therapeutic, a way to unleash and therefore heal the same childhood demons that can be cured through shrinkage.

If its attraction as an outlaw practice has been diminished, its appeal as pleasure continues to increase. Writing about the infamous French novel, *Story of O*, in which O is sadistically tortured and humiliated by her lover, French journalist Regine Deforges thought the book identified women's secret fantasies. It made "such a profound impression on those who have read it . . . ," she says to Pauline Reage, the *nom de plume* of the book's author, "because its readers, especially its female readers, recognize in it an echo of their own thoughts, of their own secret — and often subconscious — impressions. This kind of book serves to reveal to us certain truths about ourselves, and that's the kind of book that people burn."[74]

O was never burned, but it did attract the wrath of the moral authorities. In the mid-fifties, the French Book Committee, a government organization, wrote a report on the book that condemned *Story of O* as "violently and willfully immoral . . . [a book] in which the scenes of debauchery between two or even several people alternate with scenes of sexual cruelty. . . ."[75]

How much more forbidden and exciting this is than calling up an advertisement in the paper where one's darkest fantasies can be bought for $200 dollars or more. There is nothing that money can't buy, save for imagination. Susan Sontag suggested that the enduring attraction of *Story of O* lies precisely in its appeal to our minds. While most written porn has the quality of a porn movie — X fits into Y, A does such and such to B, all devoid of feeling — O is a heroine in every sense of the word. She has feelings and thoughts she describes. She establishes and maintains bonds; first with her lover René, then with Sir Stephen. The book, Sontag argues, has a defining message. Its "highest good is the transcendence of personality." It is precisely this that those involved in S/M are seeking as their ultimate reward for being bad: transcendence through pain or through a forgetting of the self in a highly ritualized sexual act that requires them to leave themselves behind and don a role. This might mean anything from one hour with someone with red nails, black high heels, and a black rubber dress, who whips you while smoking a cigarette, to a life-long commitment to be a slave, available to do a master's or mistress's every bidding at any and all times.

In their ceaseless quest for the why, the S/M optimists are not so far removed from those in the medical and psychiatric profession who pathologized these acts. The old debate about whether mixing pain and pleasure is at best reliving childhood trauma and at worst exploiting power imbalances has become just about irrelevant. Arguably, Madonna brought S/M to the mainstream with her 1994 *SEX* book. Since then, pro-sex feminists like Susie Bright have embraced S/M as play. Fashion models wear kinky leather. Weekend fetish parties are crammed with otherwise "straight" patrons looking for a walk on the wild side. Pop stars as straight-laced as soul diva Deborah Cox appear on stage in full-length leather cat suits and wrist cuffs. Porn films with S/M scenarios are becoming increasingly common. If you go to San Francisco, you may not find your heart but you can most definitely book a room at Differences, "a B&B with a difference." The B&B stands for bed and bondage and the basement houses a dungeon with metal hooks while rooms have antique bondage gear.[76] S/M for the whole family.

On a trip to a sex show held in a corporate, non-descript hotel in a suburb of Toronto, I came upon a curious scene. A young woman, dressed in a sweatsuit, was lying on a futon trying out Velcro restraints attached to the bed's four corners. People passed by and laughed as she squirmed on the bed, testing the strength of the Velcro. Meanwhile, stores offering expensive leather corsets and flogging and bondage gear are raking in the money. If you walk into Toronto's Northbound Leather, you can purchase the ultimate day-to-night wear. On its racks are conservative leather pants and jackets and tailored corsets and bustiers. When worn with a mouth harness and a fitted leather face-mask — the clothes one club attendee was sporting on a fetish night — the clothes make an S/M'er out of the most committed stockbroker.

If for most of us familiarity has bred indifference, for those who practice it, S/M has lost none of its danger and allure. Like all sex, S/M uses the body as a language and for some, S/M is the only language that allows the body to be specific about what it needs. "The obscene is a primal notion of human consciousness," Sontag argued. How can we resist?

I'm not sure what I expect when I go to Victoria's apartment. Not so long ago, another dominatrix in a Toronto suburb was charged with prostitution. (She was found guilty.) From all media accounts, her house was a bungalow on a quiet, residential street. On the other hand, when stories about dominatrixes enter the mainstream or the alternative press, they feature elaborate descriptions of black-walled dungeons outfitted with special equipment and staffed by Amazonian women. Victoria's place is a one-bedroom in a six-storey building on a quiet street a 10-minute drive from downtown Toronto. Alana lives just a few doors down. It is not the kind of apartment building that has fancy and expensive extras like a doorman, or a security intercom. You simply walk up and knock on the door of the person you're visiting.

Victoria opens the door. Behind her, a huge, sleepy St. Bernard wags its tail. Vic is wearing jeans and a t-shirt. Her voice, a deep, sexy, bored tone on the phone that is perfect for her job, is just soft in person. It has a soothing quality. She is also a nurse. This she tells me at the end of our first meeting. It seems paradoxical: by day, she alleviates pain, by night, she causes it.

"I pick up on people's pain," she says by way of explanation.

Alana is sitting on the couch smoking. When potential clients call and ask Vic to describe herself and her partner, she says of Alana that she is like Princess Xena, and she's right.

On the walls of the apartment are pictures of Vic's son, who looks to be in his mid-twenties. He doesn't know she is a part-time dominatrix, but she says that if she told him, he would probably understand.

We talk for a while about the kind of men who come to see them. Predictably enough, they cover all the bases. Married, professional men in their late thirties or early forties. Single men. Older men who have always had fantasies but have never satisfied them.

One constant is that a majority are executives.

"They're kicking people around all day, telling them what to do. They want to switch the pressure off themselves and maybe feel what it feels like," Alana explains.

She does most of the talking and despite years of being involved in S/M she still seems amazed and amused by the things people want.

One of the best stories she tells me is about a guy who has a fetish for blue tights. Unlike a dungeon, where clients come in and have a limited range of options to choose from, Alana and Vic offer what can only be described as personalized service.

In the case of the guy with the blue tights, the clock started ticking on his fantasy as soon as he parked his car in their apartment lot.

"He wanted to be taken and held prisoner," Alana says.

"We watched him park his car, and by the time he walked down the street we were behind him. He took the bag we had left for him on a mailbox, we had our regular street clothes on and PVC wear underneath, and I had a big nightstick.

"We came up behind him and we threw him to the ground. And he said 'what are you doing? what are you doing?'

"We said 'we have reason to believe you are concealing stolen property' and he had a pair of blue leotards hanging out of his pants, so we said, 'OK, that's it, we have enough evidence, we're going upstairs to take your statement.'

"He takes off his clothes and he's wearing a pair of blue tights and another pair of blue tights underneath and inside his underwear he has money and a handcuff key. We look at the handcuff key and he says he's escaped from the Don Jail for prostitution, and he's been cruising for women in his car looking for blue tights and he likes to expose himself to them."

"Do you have any idea what this guy really does?" I ask.

"Nope," Alana says and shrugs, then continues.

"He was ready to blow at any time. And we had left it so that he could escape and we said, 'OK, we're going to get some coffee,' but when we came back he was still waiting on the bed."

"He's going to come back," Vic says.

The phone rings. Victoria answers. "Yeah, hot wax, yeah. Golden showers, yeah."

"Hold on," she tells the caller.

"This guy wants two hours, the full thing. How much do we charge him?" $500, Alana tells her. "$500," Vic says into the receiver. It's a deal. Victoria gets off the phone and smiles at Alana.

"$500. Hey!" she says, before going to make us a fresh pot of coffee.

Much as some clients' fantasies are addictive, for others the thrill is in the anticipation.

"We had a guy called Antonio come in," Vic says. "And I'm standing behind him and I say 'Antonio, tell me. Tell me one of your fantasies' and he says he wants to kiss women's feet," Vic says.

"So we're on the bed and he kisses my feet and then he kisses her feet and about 12 minutes have gone by and all of a sudden he says, 'I think I've had enough, I've realized my fantasy.'"

No matter what the differences between the men are, however, one thing both women agree on is that what they are doing is a form of alternative therapy.

"If you took a Polaroid of the guys' faces when they walk in, and one when they walk out, it's like 'Phew!' like this weight has been lifted off," Vic says.

"If a guy has been bored with his sex life and he has been married for 15 years, he wants some kink, and he wants to be tied up and disciplined and dominated and you can't go to your wife after being married to her for 15 years and say 'Hon, you know what — I've been thinking a lot about wearing your panties and having you spank my ass.' They're going to say 'No, you're sick or you're perverted,'" Alana says.

Because this, after all, is S/M, a lot of the therapy involves pain. The levels involved are always just a bit higher than the ones the clients request when they come in, although Vic and Alana will not inflict so much damage as to draw blood, nor will they do anything where the client's life could be endangered.

Sometimes, though, they are amazed by the amount of pain a client can, and wants, to withstand.

"This guy came in and wanted surprise torture," Alana says.

"When you don't tell them what you're going to do, you just do it," Vic says in response to my confused look.

"Normally, you find out what levels they're at and you go with that. But this guy wanted us to do whatever," Alana continues.

"So he wanted us to retract the foreskin and drip hot wax directly on his penis. The more excruciating the better, he wanted to remember it for weeks," Alana says and shakes her head.

"And every time Alana did something, I went 'surprise!'" Victoria adds, mimicking her professional mild tone.

Had they not been involved in S/M personally, they say, they would not be able to do the job. You need to know exactly how a particular maneuver feels to be able to administer it. Victoria, however, does not tolerate any discipline.

"My father beat me black and blue," she says. "I know what pain feels like."

When Victoria says her father beat her "black and blue," I'm thrown. In my mind I instantly turn conservative: men, frankly, are swine, and women invent ever more self-destructive ways to cope with the effects of having men in their lives, and the sex industry is making money from S/M magazines and books and movies.

Perhaps it is a measure of just how acceptable S/M has become that I am far more uncomfortable with feeling this than I ever have been walking around a fetish store or watching S/M porn.

What I can't figure out, as I tell a friend later, is whether Victoria and Alana are using S/M as revenge. I myself prefer forgiveness, but that perhaps is a legacy of another kind of feminism, one that taught women to be strong, keep quiet, and put up. The one thing I do know for sure is that the more time I spend talking to Vic and Alana, the more muddled my thinking on S/M becomes and the more tepid I find the pleasure=pain equation.

I ask Vic and Alana if their feelings about men have changed since they have been involved in S/M. Alana speaks up first. For years, she says, she had been submissive in relationships, often relationships with much older men. Then one day she basically woke up and realized she didn't need to put up with being treated badly.

"I thought I should be the one that's being catered to, I should be the one that's being pampered. For me the rush is having someone come over and have them surrender to you, do anything for you," she says.

Victoria is more thoughtful about it. Right now, she is involved in a serious relationship with a submissive man.

As she talks about how her relationship is different from her professional life as a dominatrix, I think about how in some ways, she seems a lot like the clients she talks about. In her personal relationship, she can't bring herself to perform any of the things she does professionally.

The man she is with, for example, seems bossy and dominant. For one thing, he gets mad at the women if he thinks they're taking breaks. To me this sounds like he is their pimp, but both of them say that they are the ones who keep the money.

The personal relationship between him and Vic is just as troubling.

"He smashes beer bottles just so she has to clean them up," Alana says.

"Yeah, but I didn't," Victoria interjects.

Afterwards, however, he is sorry. To tell Victoria that, however, he needs to be disciplined.

"Last night we took him to a dungeon," Victoria says.

"And he was suspended and beaten for an hour," she adds and stops. "I had tears in my eyes, I wanted to go in and stop it."

"Yeah, but I told you 'He needs this, this is what he needs,'" Alana says as Victoria nods.

"Did he say he was sorry?" I ask.

"Yeah, eventually he did," Victoria says.

Wanting to be punished for doing something bad to a woman is a common theme among their clients, Alana explains.

She tells me about a man who came in because he had a bad day and had yelled at his wife. She hardly hit him before he was sobbing. Before he left, the women told him to buy a bouquet of flowers for his wife and to give it to her and to call and tell them he did as he was told. He did exactly as he was told, much to their clear satisfaction.

Of all the stories they tell me, this one is the one I keep turning over in my mind, although in its absence of sexy details, it is also the one that elicits the least amount of interest from my friends. In some ways, it gets right to the heart of the matter where S/M is concerned.

A few weeks later, I go the library to read up some more, a typical writer's block strategy. Among the stash of titles on the shelves is a book on masculinity by a gay academic. Men, he writes in a 700-page volume that goes from Clint Eastwood to Freud to Stonewall and back to Clint, are feeling threatened. Doesn't matter if they're gay or straight. From every corner they've done and are doing wrong. Sado-masochistic sexual activity has become the punishment men give themselves when they feel guilty about being unkind.

When Alana tells me the story of the man who came to them because he was unkind to his wife, I wonder what his wife would think. (If she got past the fact that he visited them in the first place.) What woman, if she were being honest, would not be flattered, moved even, by the idea of her husband feeling so awful about his treatment of her that he would take a whip? And yet what woman would want her partner to undergo physical pain, especially pain that she herself was not inflicting, and could neither control the harshness of, nor derive satisfaction from?

Then again, men have spent most of their life as a species trying and often failing to find out what it is that women want. And if women appear to be deriving great satisfaction from having men whipped, gagged, and bound, well then . . .

Sado-masochism is not just men submitting to the whims, wiles, and wills of female dominatrixes. In the on-line magazine *Salon*, journalist Julia Gracen chronicled the real-life adventures of Goreans.[77]

The Goreans take their name from the fictionalized sci-fi world created by author John Norman who wrote over a dozen books about the Planet Gor. On Gor "men are Men and women are slaves." Gracen quotes one of the books in which the narrator observes that "Slavery, of course, is the surest path by means of which a woman can discover her femininity." Not much differentiates this from the message in *Story of O*.

The Goreans are fascinating and extremely frightening. Gracen relays the substance of an e-mail she received from the real-life slave of a Gorean master in which the woman, who said she used to be a police officer and was married for 18 years, describes extraordinary deprivation and violence. "Sura [the name given to her by Master Bill] has been beaten more times than she cares to count, mostly for displeasing acts," she writes in her letter. Along with two other women she is kept in a kennel with a slave mat, blanket and footlocker for the few possessions this Bill has allowed the women to bring into his house. The Master became a member of the Gorean "lifestyle" from a BDSM discussion group and has been living this way for 14 years. Yet the women agree to this, in S/M parlance, they consent. Gracen has a troubling explanation for this, one that takes what is implied in the role-playing of the bottom in a time-limited sexual scenario to an unlimited full-time basis. Women who serve as slaves to Gorean masters, Gracen speculates, "utterly reject their former strength and self-sufficiency because they have always been unhappy with the hard necessities they experienced in taking care of themselves."

Alana and Victoria show me the bedroom. It looks like any other bedroom, a colored quilt on the bed, a shelf of books, and a dresser. The only difference is when I look at what's hanging behind the door. An assortment of whips, short-handled paddles, and canes jostle for space.

"We buy these from a riding school up north. It's cheaper than going to a fetish store," Vic says, taking a whip off the door and cracking it through the air. The sound it makes is enough to make me wince.

Victoria opens the door of the closet and pulls out a long leather dress with a zipper down the front.

"This is what I wear when clients come over," she says.

Alana is wilder in her wardrobe. At the back of the closet she has a pink gym bag. Out of it comes a short PVC dress and some garter belts and slinky black lingerie. The *pièce de résistance* is a pair of red shoes with stiletto heels and studs along the sides and heels.

"Clients seem to like these," she says with some understatement.

When I leave that first time, Victoria walks over and hugs me, then invites me to come back and watch a session. We'll say we have a new trainee, she says. Later that day at a bar, I tell a friend about the offer to sit in on the experience. If they as much as ask me to hand them a whip, I'm walking. I don't think you have to walk, he says, you can just say no. And anyway, handling a whip is not participating. Then after quite a few more drinks, he says, hey, c'mon, wouldn't you like to take a few cracks at some jerk's ass? You might find it therapeutic.

I call them Saturday and they call me back very late and Victoria leaves me a message that says they look forward to entertaining with me. I am, of course, terrified, and spend days trying to figure out where my curiosity should stop and why I feel so horrible about the whole thing.

I return a little over a week later, decked out in a PVC dress I snapped up on sale at the Bay years ago just for a kick but have never worn, black tights and black boots. I will be a good trainee. I will be called Alex.

"Did you get this stuff just for this?" they ask me.

"No, I had it," I tell them and they eye me a little suspiciously.

This time, the women aren't alone.

A gay male friend of Alana's, who works with her at her regular job as a nurse, sits in the kitchen. He fields phone calls when the women are busy in the bedroom.

The client arrives shortly afterward. He appears to be somewhere in his early to mid-thirties. He goes by the name of Steve. The first thing he says to them is to not leave any marks because he is married. He doesn't mind an observer.

We go into the bedroom. I find myself to be far less scared of what might occur than I thought I would be. Over the week afterward, I realize I blocked out the emotional impact, turning myself into a camera and simply recording what I saw.

Steve doesn't want anything out of the ordinary: bondage, anal penetration, and also to perform what is called "oral servitude" on the women.

Before he undresses, he takes off his wedding ring and puts it in his pocket.

At about the half-hour mark, I find myself yawning and looking at the books on their shelves. Unless one is a voyeur, watching other people have sex, especially people one knows in a daily context, is embarrassing. But because the activities they perform on him are also devoid of any spontaneity, it's also just as boring as reading de Sade's repetitive passages of sexual humiliation.

Apparently I'm not the only bored one. Vic looks at me and motions if I have the time. I'm not wearing a watch, so I shrug.

"Alex, can you just take over for a second?" she says, indicating the thin wood cane she is holding in her hand and walks out to check the time.

When Vic hands me the cane, I don't resist. To refuse would be to implicitly insult them, this after they volunteered to let me watch.

By the time Vic returns a few seconds later, however, some kind of transformation has taken place. I've given the guy a couple of whacks and have felt absolutely no revulsion. I cannot bring myself to hit hard enough to get the cane to make the "swish" sound Vic gets, yet I would like to, if only to prove the old "throws like a girl" adage wrong. And in my other hand I am holding a whip I grabbed off the door simply because its black leather fringes looked stylish.

She looks at me, with what I hope is some small measure of

admiration at the minute amount of courage I'm displaying, then grabs the cane back and I go off to my perch on the other side of the room.

My experiment in being a dominatrix must have lasted all of two minutes but it's made me realize two things. The first is that S/M *is* often play. Much of the fun lies in learning how to play with its toys. The other is that power, and playing with it, can become intoxicating. Steve is a mere stranger, my identity twice hidden from him, but if he was someone I knew, the small jolt of adrenaline I felt would quite likely turn to a rush — or to terror.

A few minutes later, Steve asks if Vic would like the trainee to join in.

"No, absolutely not!" Vic says in a voice that is quite unlike either her normal speaking tone, or her professional one.

No matter how far I thought I would have to go before becoming a professional dominatrix, Victoria clearly thinks it's much further. Her reaction also seems to indicate that her job does take an emotional toll on her, one that though she hardly knows me, she thinks I am best protected from.

The mood in the room breaks for a second. Alana jumps to the rescue.

"We're saving her for someone very special," she purrs and winks at me. Steve, his face down on the bed, is oblivious.

They ask him toward the end if he is enjoying himself.

"Yes, pleasing two women," he responds, then, revealing himself as an old pro, corrects himself. "I mean two mistresses. Sorry."

I think to myself how funny it is that here he is, paying $200 for an hour of S/M play, and in the end his fantasy is one of the most common of male fantasies: two women at the same time.

We go into Vic's kitchen and sit with Alana and Vic's friend afterward. No one is much disturbed.

It's only when I tell the story to friends over the following few days that I notice their interest falls somewhere between fascination and in some cases, a small amount of fear.

One time I tell the story in a restaurant and the waiter comes over right when I am describing myself holding the whip and the cane. Up to that point, he had been a friendly, smiling guy. After overhearing my conversation, he doesn't even look at me when I go up to ask for the bill.

In my friends' and strangers' reactions I find that the old questions of what emotional function S/M can serve haven't gone away. If anything, as S/M is increasingly perceived as mere child's play, they have become more acute. No longer willing to admit shame or a repulsion-fascination relationship to S/M for fear of appearing "uncool," we may very well be taming a practice that has often, for better or worse, captivated the darker recesses of the human heart.

After all, when Dominique Aury wrote *Story of O* she wrote it for her lover, the married critic Jean Paulhan, who Aury met during the Second World War. They carried on a three-decade long affair. His wife suffered from Parkinson's disease. He did not once contemplate leaving her. In her mid-40s, Aury began fearing that Paulhan might desert her for a younger woman. "I wasn't young, I wasn't pretty, it was necessary to find other weapons," she said in an interview.[78]

Aury says the stories she made up came fully formed out of her imagination. "I had the feeling that I was saying out loud something that I had been thinking for a long time. Actually, all I was trying to do was tell stories that I had so often told myself, for fun and pleasure, as I was falling asleep."[79] The stories worked. He stayed with Aury for a good many years.

CHAPTER **NINE**

HOW MUCH IS THAT WOMAN IN THE WINDOW?

I call James because I like his ad. Unlike many other ads for escort services at the back of the same Toronto weekly where I found Alana and Vic, the ad for the company he owns caters to the upscale client, a client who might just be looking for the same kind of woman I'm looking for. James's ad doesn't have a picture of a buxom woman selling her services, just a drawing of a sinuous female form.

For years, I had once in a while heard about university or college students who were working part-time as prostitutes. From what friends who knew these women said, they saw their jobs as no different than a job in a bookstore to pay the tuition. The difference between the two jobs, for them, was only in the amount of money they took home. A bookstore clerk might make $8 an hour, a little less than $60 bucks for a day's work. For an escort, $60 is said to be the minimum she would make for half an hour's work.

James's agency may be just the place to find a mythical university student. The first time I call him, I say I'm writing a book about sex. We go through some formalities. No, I'm not going to use your name, I tell him. He says he would like it if I didn't describe him either, but not because the police don't know him. They do, he says, they even wave when they see him on the street. But there are clients to consider and he doesn't want them recognizing him. OK. And no describing the girls either because that could endanger them. OK, too.

We decide to meet for lunch at a restaurant downtown. I need to know how to identify him. What do you look like, I ask. He says he'll be wearing a tweed jacket. "What about you?" he asks back. "I'm 5'6, skinny, short brown hair." I don't know what he's thinking but it occurs to me right away that these are the same rough measurements I would give him if I were applying for a job.

As soon as he gets there he wants to move from where I'm already seated. I'm sitting in the smoking section, he doesn't smoke. We move to non-smoking. He sits down and looks around. "That girl over there," his eyes move to another part of the restaurant, "the girl you were sitting beside? I'd like to hire her."

"Really? Why?"

"No, I'm just kidding," he says, laughing. "I just thought it would be a good beginning for your chapter. 'As soon as he comes in, he looks for women to hire'." He laughs again, I smile, and we start talking. (If you met him and didn't know what he did, it wouldn't occur to you that this man is a professional pimp. I feel badly even calling him that — he could be a computer techie.)

We talk for a little over an hour. At a few points in the conversation, he asks me to turn off the tape recorder. This is strange, in some ways. The things he asks me to turn the tape recorder off for are illegal, but they are in the past. The thing he is doing now is also illegal, but somehow he doesn't think he will get caught or more accurately, he expects that the police will look the other way. He tells me how many girls he has working for him — about 20. The thing he is proudest of, he says, is that he's made the business grow.

He doesn't want to do this forever, he adds, but the money will be hard to give up. How do you give up the $3000 a week in cash, the nice car, the meals, the lifestyle. Some of the girls also make $3000–$4000 a week, he says, if they work four or five nights. The agency has drivers and a receptionist. The thing about having money, he says, is it's helped him in his romantic life. It's biological. Women are programmed to look for men who have money and can provide for them and their children. They don't care where it comes from and it doesn't matter how much they make themselves. The guy should make more. Still, even with the money, at parties he doesn't really say what he does anymore. He tells his friends, but if the person doesn't know him, they're shocked though they try to hide it.

When we finish lunch, he asks me if I want to talk to some of the women. This really surprises me. I had thought we would have to meet four or five times and then eventually maybe I would dare ask to be introduced to some of them. But no, he tells me the receptionist is in the office. Just as we are about to leave, his cell phone rings. One of his employees is calling in. I can hear her voice and it's high and girly and nothing like my own voice and that's why she's getting $3000 a week and I'm not, I think. Very quickly you realize just how fast it is to get accustomed to what everyone does for a living. I'm just comparing salaries — I've already forgotten what it is she does.

"I've got a $3000 gig for you," he says. "Yup. A few days in California. In July. Six girls. How do I know why he wants six girls? I didn't ask him that. He's a guy who has a computer company. I didn't ask him why he wants six girls." The woman on the other end is asking more questions. He cuts her off, "I'll call you later, OK?"

He tells me her name and explains that she is at the top range of the business. He doesn't buy that his women are selling sex out of necessity. Some of them are, sure. But they are not walking the streets and most aren't using the money for drugs. Need is a tricky proposition, he says. Do you really need the fancy car and the condo and the nice clothes? If you want it, then maybe you need it, but that's not the same as saying that you need the money for food. Women who truly need the money, on the other hand, can be his favorite employees. What he particularly likes is when women come in who have children. It means they are more stable. Not only are they more likely to stick around, they are more responsible. Is that a concern, I ask. Women just quitting on you, or not being reliable. His answer is interesting.

"In this business, being reliable and responsible is different," he says. "At a regular job, if you're half an hour late, or if you miss some shifts, you get fired. But if a girl shows up three out of four shifts, she's really responsible."

"So you let them take nights off if they need to?"

"I have to. It's not just another job. If they're not up to it they're not. You have to be up for it."

Few people that the women are friends with know what they do for a living. A few times he's gone to a restaurant and run into women who work for him or who have worked for him in the past. They look like anyone else and they mutually ignore each other.

Then he talks about the clients. Women, he thinks, would never pay for sex. But for some reason, men have no problem. A lot of them have wives, have corporate jobs, others drive trucks or whatever. In every way, they span the range — about 50 per cent of customers on any night are from out of town. And about 30 per cent are repeat customers. That doesn't mean they want the same girl, but they use the same company. The money is always up front. The women also get tips. He doesn't ask them about the tips. That's for them to take.

We pay and walk out. I think to myself that this is where this can get scary. I ask him how far the office is. He says only about ten minutes. Then we get into his car, which I'm not happy about. But in the car he tells me he's reading a book of essays by a dead obscure filmmaker. As it turns out, James majored in fine arts in university. We talk about the dead obscure filmmaker until we get to the office. We go in and he introduces me to a very pretty girl, dressed in black who looks to be about 20. She's the receptionist and her name is Sarah. Someone else is there to apply for a job and a friend of Sarah's is sitting smoking with her. The friend sometimes works for the agency but not very often.

I talk to Sarah while James goes to interview the new applicant, a tall, leggy blonde with big hair and lots of make-up and a push-up bra that you can see through her thin white sweater. She has worn, form-fitting clothes and looks to be anywhere between 19 and 27.

Sarah answers the phones and types in customers' most frequent requests, both for what they want sexually and which girls get the most repeat business. She also records where the calls come from. Are they from the airport hotels, or are they from downtown? This agency only does outcalls; no client can come to a girl's house. The information is processed on an on-going basis so that she can tell me how popular "Greek style" is, and then cross-reference that information against the preferences of out-of-towners and against the girls they request. It's like the Kinsey report of johns on her computer except it's not terribly useful from a business perspective. The agency doesn't ask the women what they do and doesn't negotiate with clients on activities; they listen to what the men want and then tell them what they do in the privacy of their hotel rooms is their business. All they provide is a lady to keep you company for the evening. In practice, this means the women can negotiate higher fees once they are with a client.

It's still pretty quiet, since it's early afternoon and the phone doesn't start ringing until about 3:30. Sarah says she started out working for James by being an escort. She did it about three times and couldn't do it anymore. Before that, she had drug problems, she ran away from home, she lived on the street. I ask her why with all the skills she has now, all of which she taught herself, why she wouldn't consider getting a job in the straight world? After all, she modernized the office. It was her idea to keep statistics. She tells me she couldn't, she has a grade 10 education. Everything she's learned about office work, she's learned with James.

Since she dropped out, she can tell which girls aren't suited to the job from the moment they walk in the door. How do you know, I ask her. They ask the wrong questions, she says. They want to know what the guy is going to want, and can they say no, and most of all, they ask if the guys ever say no, I don't like this girl, I want another girl. In other words, they want to know if they will be rejected. Sarah says you can't be like that in this business. She, here she points to her friend who hasn't said anything at all, got rejected three times in one day. And she came back and held her head high and said, who's next?

I look over at the woman and she's pretty as well, maybe a little tired, and she nods. "Yeah, it's true."

So these guys are really specific about what they want? And if you're not providing it, then they send the girl back? Oh yeah, Sarah tells me. She says she has lots of respect for the women who do this, because she knows. But when the ones who are nervous get in, she wants to just tell them not to, but she can't do that. They get their hearts broken, she says. I think that I've always believed that if their hearts weren't already broken before they found themselves facing Sarah, they wouldn't be there. Lately, I'd been reconsidering that and think that maybe at least some of these women have hearts that are well guarded against this sort of thing. They're professionals.

The phone calls start trickling in. Most of the callers are asking for specific women. Is so and so in? When is she working next? It's like calling for a date with the high-school cheerleader. Sarah tells them when the girls get into their shift and whether or not they're working that evening. As the day wears on, calls from new customers come in.

Right now, Elizabeth, and Chayenne and Toni are on duty. Sarah describes each of the women. She gives their measurements. The guys want to know more. Sarah tells them that one woman has a nice smile, another is mulatto, lovely skin, a third is very beautiful. Her voice is so mellow that it sounds patient and soothing.

At the back of the office there are photo lights and a white screen, it's for the girls to get their photos taken for the service's web site. Later on, I check out the photos on-line, their faces are all blanked out, but their bodies are indeed perfect.

James tells me he will introduce me to some of the women. "Do you really want to know how this business works?" he asks. He sounds really sincere. I tell him I do. He shakes his head, maybe he doesn't know why I want to know and if he asked me, at this moment I couldn't answer him. On the way out, I ask Sarah to give me a call and shake her hand and everything that I've ever read by feminists about how prostitution is bad for women comes rushing at me and I want to take her home and feed her and get her into a graphic design program at Sheridan College or something.

About a week later, I meet Sarah for a drink. She arrives on a bike, looking frail and wearing a hooded sweatshirt and a pair of jeans. She's changed out of her more grown-up work outfit and now looks just like any other kid on the street. I ask her questions about the business, but the openness that was there in the office has faded and she is reluctant to answer. She wants to know more about how come I'm writing a book and how do you do that and it strikes me that she is resisting what I'm trying to do to her which is turn her into just another example of someone who works in the sex industry. She does tell me that the amounts James said the women make are inflated; that no woman can work the hours it would take to make that kind of money a week. Maybe for a few days, but for a month? No. She also talks a lot about how terrible she felt when she did work as an escort briefly. Then I kind of give up trying to interview her. This is a girl I have nothing in common with, but for no other reason than that I was born in a different family than she was. We chat a bit about nothing in particular, how school was, music — then I tell her to call me if she wants to talk. I'm not sure what purpose is served by harassing a woman to give up her time to me so that I can engage in some second-hand sociological observation. If anyone should be writing about the daily lives of prostitutes, it's the women themselves.

It's not the first time I've felt like this, vaguely dirty not for looking into how prostitution works, but for getting the thrills for free without ever doing anything about improving these women's experiences. Liberal guilt is a sickening thing to observe in oneself, and probably more tiresome to hear about. Still, it's been with me for years.

Our taboos against prostitution are such that the idea of a woman taking money for sex means that whenever people mentioned knowing such a woman they would either do so dismissively, or if they thought of themselves as liberal, with a small, confused frown. Two thousand years after Mary Magdalene prostitution is still unclean, something that women, given the chance to make the same amount of money elsewhere, would avoid.

What was always interesting to me about the frown that accompanied mention of the moonlighting students is that if anyone should be considered able to make those decisions, if anyone should at the very least not look as if they were in need in rescuing, it would be university students. These women were said to always work for escort services. They did not stand on street corners in the bitter cold; they were driven to appointments by the agency's drivers, thereby lessening the danger, and being young and beautiful they would command the highest wages. Because of all this what would have normally been pity or discomfort turned to confusion. Why would a well-educated woman with a professional future of some kind ahead of her resort to prostitution, "resort" being the operative term.

Over the years, however, as these women were mentioned — and everyone seemed to have known of one at some point — that confused frown became colored with envy. Women in particular were often in awe of the money. "They make so much money!" The implied and not said question always hovered in the air, expressed only among the best of friends. "Would you ever do that?" and its logical companion, "How could you do that?"

These conversations took place once in a while over the years I was in university. No one had actually spoken to these university students. But the rumors continued unabated, just as college campuses were becoming the supposed hotbeds of politically correct feminist radicalism. The existence — real or imagined — of these women, could only be explained by the still apparent lack of women in top professional jobs. Until women became visible in positions of power and wealth, the world's oldest profession would continue to be an attractive career option. No one could see prostitutes as anything other than victims.

I was willing to believe that women would not willingly prefer prostitution over life as say, a highly paid corporate lawyer, but I also did not want to see them as victims. To do so would be to perpetuate the same kind of feminism that had for a long time discounted the experiences of women from less developed countries, as if a lack of education amounted to a lack of wisdom. So I thought at the time; I did not want to force any woman into the white, liberal, and privileged cookie cutter I was living in. If these women were victims, it was not their lack of education or their attendant poverty that doomed them, but the archaic conservatism of a society that could not bear admitting it supported a thriving sex industry. Otherwise why not legalize it and free the women who sold sex from the real dangers of their job: street-walking, pimps, cops, and the drug trade.

So I interviewed a few prostitutes for a story for the campus paper, several of them activists for the legalization of prostitution. The women told me their stories, how they started, where they were living and why they needed prostitution legalized. At one point during the project, I met three of the women I was talking to for Sunday brunch. What I didn't say in the published piece was this.

Halfway through brunch, one of the women who had been looking pale from the beginning, got up and excused herself to go to the bathroom. When she returned, she was alive again. Whatever she had done in the bathroom, she'd badly needed to do it. Was she in that kind of shape because she was a prostitute, or was she a prostitute because her life had led her to solutions that caused as much pain as the sorrow she wanted to obliterate? I didn't know then, nor did I stop to consider it very long. I was so concerned with making sure my article didn't exploit the women by re-victimizing their lives, that I could barely see the reality in front of me. They were victims.

So several years later I was still looking for the prostitute in charge of her life, the pretty woman who didn't need or want to be rescued from a life of sin because she wasn't sinning. I don't think I'm alone among feminist women in hoping to find her. A woman should be able to sell her sexual services without stigma. The transaction would be purely commercial, the only discussions accompanying it focused on safe sex and marketing yourself. Topics could range from knowing how to spot dangerous johns, to how to maintain your health, to interior decorating, to props, to costumes, to ensuring repeat business. That's not the world we live in.

In the fall of 1998, author Mary Gaitskill came to give a talk at Toronto's annual Authors' Festival. In her short stories and her novel, *Two Girls, Fat and Thin*, Gaitskill has dissected all the petty meanness of casual relationships. You could say she's a profoundly cynical writer, or you could say she's realistic. At a certain point in my life what she had to say about the wanton and careless cruelty of humans said something to me about my own life; these days I think perhaps, as writer Elizabeth Wurtzel says, that we are all capable of being better than the worst things that ever happened to us. Gaitskill herself was once, and very briefly, a stripper in Toronto. As it rapidly became clear during her post-reading interview with Toronto author Lynn Crosbie, this is a part of her past she does not want re-visited

Just a few days before, a local weekly had run a profile of Gaitskill. In it, the reporter had linked Gaitskill's writing with her personal history. Reading the piece, she had felt it was a violation: her past had been used as a selling tool, a sexy bit of information that teased the reader into the story. The information also made what she had been doing with her hands for many years less important than what she had done with her body for a few months years ago.

Then she said something else. Right now, she said, in San Francisco, women are talking of being strippers or escorts as if it was a new fad. Women, she added, who don't have to do it, who have educations (who unlike Gaitskill herself at the time she was in the business), have other financial choices. These women, she was suggesting, were being sadly misled if they thought that they were at all empowering themselves.

Sex is trendy enough, however, that becoming the person who sells it can seem at times like a way to celebrity. Interviews with porn stars are featured in mainstream magazines and some of the most talked about female singers have taken the selling of sex as their mantra. This book doesn't have the word "sex" in the subtitle for nothing — in a sea of publishing every bit helps.

Gaitskill's reaction to women who freely choose to work as prostitutes is a quaint reminder of another era. Offered the choice between being movie stars and porn stars, how many women would really choose the latter? Yet no one makes judgments anymore — after all, it's far more comfortable to ironically consume images of naked men and women than to admit to being truly titillated, no matter what the consequences for the people whose images we hunger for.

A few months pass after my drink with Sarah. She doesn't call me and I don't pursue it. Plus, at this point I've decided that since I'm not offering them friendship (not that they would want it necessarily) if I'm going to be interviewing sex trade workers, I'll pay for their time just like their clients have to. Meanwhile, a friend is working on a novel. She imagines the lead character being a stripper and one conversation leads to another and we decide that in the interests of research we're going to go to a strip club. She'll try and talk to the women who work there to flesh out her character; I'll observe the selling of sex in one of the places where it's most openly practiced.

Over the course of a couple of weeks we hit three strip clubs. A strange thing happens: we end up liking them just as places to hang out. They're relatively quiet, no one bothers you or looks at you unless you look at them, and the clubs are lit only by diffuse pink and blue lights. The space between tables is big enough that no one can hear a private conversation. I can't imagine a better place to conduct mergers and takeovers, or if we were characters in *The Sopranos*, arrange mob hits.

One evening, we ask for a table dance and proceed to interview the woman stripping in front of us. She sits down and chats instead. Much as we suspected, women are her favorite customers: they don't try and touch, they tip well and they're "nice." One unexpected result of attending these clubs is that we both feel as if we've overcome some invisible barrier by invading what is usually considered "men-only space." The sense of power aside, exactly what we've won by going where we haven't been invited isn't terribly clear to me.

Does our presence say to the men 'You can buy other women, but we know what you're doing and who you are?' 'You can buy women, but so can we?' 'We don't care if you buy women, we are not taking our clothes off?' Anyway, though the clubs cater to men, our money is as good as anyone's and so maybe it's not so surprising that we are only hassled at the door once. The bouncer wants to see I.D. We're flattered that we must look so young and we explain the academic purpose of our research. "Oh, OK," he says. "Sorry, it's just that a lot of hookers come in here." Ah. He thought we were looking for potential clients.

News of our "escapades" reaches a reporter who is writing a story about women who go to strip clubs for entertainment. We don't quite fit the bill but we're good enough for the purpose of the article. A story appears shortly after.[80] It hits every angle: women conquering men's territory, not being afraid to look, removing the stigma of selling sex and turning its sale into just another form of entertainment. Wow, my friend and I are part of a movement I didn't even know existed. Reading the story feels like hollow liberation. The women interviewed in the story and the ones I talk to on our nights out aren't talking about unionizing or better working conditions. Having women customers instead of men is as good as it gets apparently. And not a single one of us is saying any different, as if we've learnt the lesson of Third Wave feminism — thou shalt not accuse another female of false consciousness but instead respectfully listen and nod as she retells her experience — all too well.

By the time I find someone else who feels as uncomfortable with what happened as I do, it's again several months later at an office Christmas party. The woman I talk to is a columnist who I think is in her late thirties or early forties. Unprompted, she asks me what I thought of the article about women going to strip clubs? I tell her I was one of the women and I still haven't quite decided what I think of the whole thing. She has no doubts: here were a bunch of privileged, educated women simply taking advantage of another group of women happy for the small amount of respect and extra tips. There are no post-modern nuances in her analysis, no talk of university students choosing to strip for enlightenment, and no forgiving the detached stance of the young women who thought to find themselves by forgetting about someone else. It's old-style feminism and she is so right.

In Lisa Palac's *The Edge of the Bed*, the author rebounds from a failed romance by hiring two male prostitutes to visit her and her friend (renowned sex author Susie Bright) in a Las Vegas hotel room. They are specific when hiring the duo, they want large, athletic and preferably bisexual. And if they don't like what comes through the door? They vow to send them back. Women, obvious as it is to state it, do not account for as large a share of the sex-for-sale market as men do. So when they do buy, they make a big fuss about how they're going to be assertive. But in the end, even though the men are not bisexual, the women don't complain and Bright even ends up more concerned about whether the boys have a good time than whether she is.

But I think there is something else to the two's discomfort. Years spent in the trenches of the sex-positive movement may not make it easier to reconcile the quest for pleasure with the realization that for those in the sex trade, pleasure is just another word for earning a living. Can you really free your body when the people helping you do so feel nothing of the sort?

Sex is a marketplace. In 1979, some 1000 titles were available on home video. By 1990, after the porn industry switched to filming on video, 5000 titles were available. In the last several years, that output has gone to 5000 titles a year and Americans are renting 100 million X-rated tapes a year. Some statistics suggest that 40 per cent of those who rent these tapes are women.

The hideous excesses of which it is capable aside (such as the *Houston 500* gang bang video), porn is the one place where women are not chastised for being horny, where the word nymphomaniac is not a threat, where the slut has only good rumors spread about her. And she gets the boy too. A woman in a mainstream film first has to play it cool, to be a bitch, to even lose the guy before she gets him. In other words, her desires have to be masked, twisted, repressed.

This is why Candida Royalle and Annie Sprinkle have made porn for women, porn in which the women have real breasts and the camera focuses as much on the woman's face at the moment of her orgasm as on the "money shot." Sometimes the women porn makers even forgo the money shot. But most women don't live in places where you can rent these videos at the corner video store. They don't live in New York, or Toronto, or Montreal, or Los Angeles, or San Francisco. Most women live in places where Blockbuster is the video store of choice, where the mainstream rules, where a woman can't be seen crawling across the floor to give her man a blow job unless she is either being made to do it or is after something like else, like a ring or his wallet.

So looked at in this way, some porn can be positive, empowering even. Its liberation, however, is a product. It can be fun to watch, it can momentarily make us lose our inhibitions, but it can't change our selves. Behind the fight to have sex toys sold in Alabama, behind opposition to Canadian government legislation to seize at the border any material that links sex and violence, behind every emporium of adult videos and paraphernalia and every hip, feminist sex toy and education store, behind every club night devoted to a fetish/leather theme, is a business. Put this way, there isn't much difference between a woman calling herself Candy and advertising herself as a shaved 18-year-old with size D breasts, her picture calling out to the lonely guy in the middle of the night from the back of *Rolling Stone* magazine and available for $10 a call (that would be to say hello; anything after that is $1.99 a minute) and the pen and ink drawing of a curvaceous, womanly shape, hippie wild hair seemingly blowing in the wind, who is the mascot for Good for Her, a Toronto store that is the epitome of discretion, taste, and feminine empowerment when it comes to the selling of sex toys.

I go into Good for Her one summer afternoon on my way home. It's quiet. A sign on the door advertises that on one afternoon a week the store is open to women only. A few times a month the store offers seminars on sexuality, from safe S/M to how to conduct a polyamorous relationship.

Wooden shelves in the store hold a variety of toys, from small, hand-held vibrators, to plastic rubber duckies shaped for pleasure, to mammoth dildos going for almost $200 each. Each of the products has a rating from the staff on its power, efficiency, subtlety: bang for the buck. Candida Royalle's vibrators are the prettiest, in pink, yellow, and green. They come in a non-sexual shape that fits the palm of your hand. Pretty much everything else resembles a penis, except for vibrating balls. Another set of shelves has a small selection of porn movies, most of them made by women; another books, evenly divided between instructional, art, and erotic literature. Plants dominate everything. They cover up the front window and are scattered throughout the store making me think that perhaps Good for Her could start a sideline business as a greenhouse.

The woman who is working behind the counter is lovely. She offers to help me and when I say I'm just browsing, retreats and ignores me as I pick up each item and check out its speeds, rhythm, color, and shape. I can't actually tell the difference between anything until I've tested them against my hand at least three times. There's no hard sell here. A woman comes in and picks up a video on her membership, then leaves quietly.

A couple walk in. One half of the couple is a woman who used to go out with a friend of mine. She and her friend start looking at some toys. When she looks at me, I smile back but she ignores me and pretends not to know me. I'm offended a little bit, but on the other hand, her reaction is understandable. Only someone who's been thinking and writing about sex for two years would feel otherwise. Choosing a sex toy is an incredibly private thing — when WASPs do it, they write away for the Xandria catalogue they see advertised at the back of *Harper's* magazine, the one which assures the sexually-liberated academic set that they will receive their catalogue and their purchases in brown wrapping paper. So why would we stop in the middle of the store to have a chat? Just because sex is freely available, it doesn't necessarily mean we've been freed. Or that we truly want to be.

A few months before my visit to Good for Her, I'd gone to a Tupperware party with a twist. The same friend who was hosting this party had just a while before thrown a real Tupperware party. So successful was the first venture — the Tupperware lady begged her to sign on as a rep after she'd made almost $1000 in sales in just two hours — that Karen had now branched out into home sex toys. The front room of the house where the party was being held was headquarters for a sensual-looking woman dressed in a long blue dress. She sat on the floor, her knees tucked under her. On a blanket were arranged a selection of toys similar to the ones available at Good for Her. The first order of business, however, was to loosen up the guests. Each of us was given a piece of paper on which we were asked to write down one sexual fantasy and also the dirtiest thing we'd ever done. The only man in the room quickly retreated. About three-quarters of the women rapidly followed him.

Didn't matter that the attendees for this party were a Benetton ad for sexual flexibility, every sexual stripe represented. We may have come prepared to drop some cash for sex hardware, but we did not want to talk to each other about it. I think there is a lot of this confusion: between the ever-expanding sexual marketplace and the private liberation that people feel, or not. Because couples can be found loudly arguing over which porn flick to see tonight at the local non-Blockbuster video store and women can choose from ten different colors of dildo to share (or not) with their lover, our sexual mores are thought to be just as liberal. I'm not sure there is a relationship between the two, or if there is, perhaps it is one of inverse relations.

We are not fuller citizens because we have 10 possible cellular plans to chose from any more than we are sexual agents because we can choose between Japanese, German, Swedish, or English porn videos. Much as I'm opposed to the censoring of sexual materials in the interests of morality, I don't believe making sex and its depiction more easily available is the road to personal sexual nirvana either.

There is only one segment of society that truly benefits from the explosion of sex materials, the sex industry. *Hustler* became famous when it published nude pictures of Jacqueline Kennedy Onassis. Larry Flynt bought the photos for $18,000, the magazine sold a million copies. For the rest of us, it's just entertainment, the spicy version of playing on a Sony Playstation on a Saturday night. Flynt knows this. "That's the thing to getting people in — you make them feel they're in a Neiman-Marcus or Barnes and Noble," he said in a newspaper article. "All of a sudden, it's not dirty anymore."[81]

When the 1939 World Fair opened in New York, it included *Dream of Venus*, a Salvador Dali-designed installation in which girls nude to the waist swam past melting watches and played with giant rubber telephones. Meanwhile, a local minister criticized it because it presented a "menace to morals." Outside the fair, mayor Fiorello La Guardia sentenced three men to jail time because they had wanted to hold a Miss Nude 1939 at the fair. In one of the first successful sex ventures, millions turned out for the event.

A certain kind of sex is becoming separate from morality — precisely that kind of sex which is for sale. Prostitution, Internet sex shows, porn videos; all are being sold as legitimate products. Censoring them would deprive adults of their rights as consumers. The people providing these services haven't risen in our esteem, however. Like the underpaid wage slaves who work at McDonald's, they are seen at best as exploited, at worst as not smart enough to get a better job. It's no accident that the most widely available sex services on the Internet advertise the women who work for them as hookers, porn stars and sluts. "Sexual freedom has so often been more easily interpreted as some sort of consumer sale-a-thon, 'Get'cher red hot vibrator and filthy movie delivered Federal Express before 10 a.m. the next morning,'" says Susie Bright. True erotic liberation, she insists, isn't as easily digested: "It's frightening because it insists that not everyone is meant to offer the same things, to be the same way in the world."[82] I would add that it also insists that we make our choices about where we want to fit in every day and respect the choices of others. So simple and yet so murderously difficult in practice.

When it comes to private sexual behavior, few of the taboos and shame-inducing restrictions on sexuality have truly budged in decades. As we have had the opportunity to sample more and more sex products, have we become any less judgmental and repressive about the kind of morality we will sanction in private life?

Sexually aggressive women are demonized, those who deviate from the two-gender world shunned, and the sexual lives of our public figures a moral bellwether by which we take the measure of their character. Alarm attaches to most discussions of adolescents' sexual development. Is is almost as if having glimpsed new sexual possibilities in the myriad choices available to us in the sexual marketplace, we have become terrified that those possibilities might invade our lives.

We have seen the enemy and it is us.

I don't think it's a coincidence that growing numbers of people seem willing to engage in vigilante actions against pedophiles at the same time that thousands of Internet sex sites advertise their wares as "barely legal." Fear is giving rise to the hard-line rhetoric of moral sex crusaders; fear that if we stop looking over our shoulder, someone is going to catch us staring at the images we want to burn. Could it be otherwise? Could we live in our current climate — inundated by sexual imagery in real and virtual life — and not imagine it as a threat? I think so. Minds, not bodies, are the most powerful weapons in the arsenal we have to become truly at peace with our desires.

Imaginations are the only tool we have to truly revolutionize our relationship to our sexuality and our bodies so that shame would no longer attach to either. Sex would become a private matter again — between a person and her partner, or partners. Until that day, sex will make even the bravest among us blush and the sex industry will continue to sell us other people's misery under the guise of consumer freedom.

CHAPTER **TEN**

I DO

There is no more lovely, friendly and charming relationship, communion or company than a good marriage.

— Martin Luther[83]

Early in the evening, my grandmother sits in a padded chair at her polished dark mahogany dining room table. The tabletop is covered in protective layers: long, broad sheets of tissue paper, a clear plastic cover, a white tablecloth and in the places where her and my grandfather sit, two placemats. The only way to know the table is made of wood is to bend down and look at the legs, or to have been there decades ago when the table was uncovered every Sunday, when they still hosted Sunday lunches for their family and friends, a time before their son, his wife, and their two children moved a continent and an ocean away.

There are still six chairs around the table. Galina sits in the one closest to my grandfather. He is seated at the head of the table, reading that day's newspaper through a large, hand-held magnifying glass. I'm in the seat next to her. It's the first time I've sat there in the 16 years since the December my mother, my brother, and I left Romania to join our father who had immigrated to Canada.

We're chatting (I don't remember about what, probably about the country's rising prices and declining pensions). We're speaking quietly because somehow this makes it easier to be heard over the din of the suppertime news. The volume of the television is turned up high so that my grandfather, who is losing his hearing, can hear. I've never been a fan of the power television has to distract humans from each other and I'm losing my patience.

"Can I turn this down?" I ask my grandfather.

"What?" he responds.

"The TV," I say.

"What?" he says again without looking up from his paper.

"Where is your hearing aid?" my grandmother says to him, her head beginning to shake in exasperation.

"What?" he responds again and this time looks up, just in time to see Galina shuffle off her chair, gather her housecoat about her, and go in search of the magic device. She returns holding it without its case.

"Mishulica, Mishulica," she says, calling him by her pet name for my grandfather's Mihail. "What am I going to do with you?"

He grins happily at her, takes it from her hand and sticks it in his ear. "I hear like a youngster," he says.

She stands silently above him, frowning. "Turn it on, Mishulica," she says and reaches behind his ear. He turns it on.

I start laughing. He does too. Then he pats her bum.

She passes away only a few months later, just before Christmas. My father and I have dinner and talk about the kind of trouble my headstrong grandfather is already stirring up without her tempering influence around. He wants to sell their apartment, he claims he needs no help, he forgets to turn off the gas stove at night and leaves the water running in the bathroom. Already the tub has overflowed and destroyed the ceiling of the neighbors' flat below.

We only talk about how my grandfather must feel, as opposed to the trouble he's causing, once.

"I remember when I was there," my father says, talking about when he visited his parents a year before. "She said to me, 'I only wish the house was a little bit more joyful.' Can you imagine? Only that the house be more joyful."

I understand what my grandmother must have meant. Everyone has had their share of tiptoeing around someone else, hoping the fog they are enshrouded in might lift, hoping there would be laughter. That was not what I'd seen when I was with them, I say to my father. They seemed all right. Perhaps I had closed my eyes, seen only what I'd wanted to see, a quiet, long marriage that in its later years was contented, if only because they had been left with no one else from whom to draw contentment. Looked only at her finding his hearing aid, him patting her bum. To me, it looked like joy.

"Some people would be better off divorced." The phrase trips off my tongue easily, slipping out as I talk to a friend about marriages we know of where the principals have been clawing at each other since the wedding day. "It may have been better for me," he says, referring to his own parents' marriage, "it may have been better for me if they hadn't stayed together." How do you know? I ask him. It could have been better, but it also could have been worse. Ever since the advent of more liberal divorce laws, studies have seesawed on the effects on the children. For people around my generation — those who grew up from the late seventies to the mid-eighties — divorce among parents is so common as to not merit any surprise. And yet the older couples among our parents who have stayed together are studied, examined, talked about. What is it that they know that other parents did not know? In the face of the widespread failure of so many partnerships, a lot of young people have retrenched, living together instead of going to church in the white dress. What is the point of getting married if it is going to fail?

The hunger for knowing how to make it work, though, doesn't go away. If divorce is one of the most common shared stories, marriage is the fairy tale that's nice to read about but seemingly impossible to realize. Since 1960, the marriage rate has dropped by 43 per cent in the United States, and popular culture become strewn with portrayals of marriage as a project which inevitably comes to a bitter end. "The fraud factor is what Paul calls it, the fear of being revealed," writes

A.M. Homes in her 1999 novel *Music for Torching*, a story about a fragmented marriage that destroys the family at its core. The trouble is apparent when the book's couple wordlessly agree to set their home on fire. "Paul and Elaine already knew it, and in fact, setting the fire was on some level a declaration of their awareness, the great and formal announcement: This is not who we are, we are not like you, we have failed, we are failing, we are failures. And yet, this is exactly who they are; they are not different at all. They are exactly the same as everyone else, and worse yet, they are trapped in it, entirely engulfed — this is their life."[84]

And what of the portrait of marriage in *American Beauty*? I saw it when it came out, on a blazing hot summer afternoon. With a friend, I huddled in the chill air of one of those super air-conditioned movie theaters. There were only a few other people there with us; this was maybe the first or second week it was on, before it had become an unlikely mainstream hit. As Kevin Spacey's maniac attempt to propel himself out of stasis and his neighbour's son's methodical attempts to record every moment of grace in a not-so-barren world went on, I felt a burning chill enter my heart. The movie left me very sad, probably partly because the lost possibilities it depicted are so close to those in our world.

Annette Bening, on the other hand, made me angry. I could understand the impulse behind wanting to bury yourself in a fascist version of Martha Stewart to keep your emotions at bay. I could even understand how an affair with a cold, big-toothed real estate agent could seem like an exit. What I didn't understand is why the compassion extended to the other characters was not extended to her and why, by extension, compassion was withheld precisely from the relationships in the movie where time and intimacy and wisdom should have made it most present: from marriage.

Instead the key marriages in the movie were more than sterile. These unions were indicted as the crucible of the destruction of the soul. What had happened between the time when Spacey and Bening had fallen in love and had children, to the time when she repulses his attempt at sex on the couch because the sofa is too precious a designer item? Why was the only way out for one of them to die? Like *The Ice Storm* a couple of years before, the most critically successful movies of the late 1990s banked on the idea that marriage was in irreparable disrepair, just another symptom of society's fall. It left out how we had gotten there.

Ironically, the parents that got divorced in such record numbers are the same ones who fret over their lack of grandchildren and their children's lack of permanent ties in their life. As Larissa Philips said in an article explaining why her boyfriend and her aren't trading up from cohabitation, "The aging boomers seem shocked and befuddled that someone would choose to avoid the whole swampy mess of broken vows and failed traditions they've left in their wake."[85]

About the only place to find a defense of marriage is among conservative pundits, who to me always smell suspicious. I don't trust them not to throw out decades of human rights gains. For them, sending women back to the kitchen and making divorce more difficult will solve everything. To conservatives, the great stain of North American society is not in that society's failure to marshal its resources to protect its weak, but in the failure of men and women to stay together. "For the sake of the children" is invoked as a way to revoke the rights of the adults.

Just last summer, a group calling itself The Marriage Movement issued a report on the state of marriage. "Marriage," it said, "is a universal human institution, the way in which every known society conspires to obtain for each child the love, attention, and resources of a mother and a father." Among their other proposals was a plan to link all government-funded teenage sexual education programs to schools teaching abstinence. Another number of words is devoted to vague advice such as "deepen your commitment to the marriage promise."

The over three dozen people who put their name to the statement include the highly regarded psychologist Judith Wallerstein. Last fall, Wallerstein was much criticized for *The Unexpected Legacy of Divorce.* The book renewed the debate in the United States as to whether marriage is the cure for all that ails us. Decades ago, Wallerstein began following several dozen children whose parents had split up. In the current book, she interviewed those among them who were still willing to talk about their lives. The worst effects of their parents' break-ups were felt in adult life, she claims. Romances failed because the grown-up children felt that no situation was worth resolving because the love would end anyway.

As it turns out, the book's methodology is disastrously flawed. Katha Pollitt, for example, argues that the families Wallerstein studied had troubles far deeper than just divorce. The families, Pollitt writes, feature "crazy parents, economic insecurity, trapped wives and, as Wallerstein does discuss, lots of violence (one-quarter of the fathers beat their wives; out of the 131 children, 32 had witnessed such attacks)."[86]

The battle over Wallerstein's data just shows me what I have always suspected. When it comes to intimate relationships the only thing that matters is the stories we have told ourselves.

Between images of marital dissolution and confusion and the messages of conservative politicians who righteously fulminate against love outside the law, there must be a middle ground where our imaginations reign. To me, this would be a place where romance can thrive in spite of the absence of any illusions except that of the beauty of the every day. What I have are the stories of the marriages I have seen and heard about around me. Some are bad, some are good — most of us persist in trying to create a life with another human being.

Lesbian women and gay men are demanding the right to marry because so powerful is the urge to mate with another that for society to deny that right to some is a denial of their humanity. Right-wing opponents of same-sex marriage are missing out. If anyone could help advance their belief in the importance of marriage and family, in marriage as a sacred institution to be aspired to, it's those in the gay and lesbian community who are pushing for amorous equality under the law. Without the same kind of community pressure that heterosexuals face, gays and lesbians still want the option of having their union with another human being sanctified by state, and church.

So in one form or another, marriage as an idea has endured. Plato thought "marriage should not be a mere association for the purpose of perpetuating the species but an alliance of two reciprocally affectionate and tender persons which may perfectly well meet every moral need of humanity."[87] Perhaps it is no longer this — the primary social institution — perhaps it will never regain that status. But then should a union of two individuals recognized by their family and friends replace that family and those friends? There's only one path that has the potential to reveal whether anyone can salvage the spiritual, emotional and intellectual challenges of marriages from its death rites: one of persistence, faith and not a small dose of reality.

My parents are one of the few married couples I know closely who have stayed together for decades; that could always change. Theirs is not a model marriage — but then I don't think any marriage can be. Since I was a child, I wondered on-and-off if continuing in it was always the best thing for them. Lately, though, I've realized that in their own way they have taught me something about the mystery at the heart of any marriage that endures. In the face of all the evidence around me, the broken vows, the terrible pain that divorce inflicts on the people parting (not just on children), it feels quaint (maybe even foolish) to me to try and argue that promising to spend one's life next to another's is still worthwhile. In many ways, it goes against everything else that is in this book — since so many of these pages are about finding ways to personal freedom. But if liberty lies in love, then marriage at its most fulfilling can be the freest place on Earth.

I could, of course, use pseudonyms, or a hypothetical friend's parents, or a real friend's parents. As concert groupies might put it, though, where my parents are concerned, I had backstage access. Undoubtedly, my memories have been edited according to the limits of my imagination — the truth of it is known only to them. I have never asked about the incidents that troubled me and in a way perhaps I don't need to know. What I remember is what has shaped me and I'm not sure revising those memories according to fact will re-shape me in a better mold.

When I was younger I remembered the bad parts far more. As time has worn on, and as the years when I lived at home recede further into the past, I have not forgotten about the rows, but those memories have become less important than my increasing curiosity at how they have stayed together for over 30 years. How two people who for as long as I remember have threatened to divorce each other have nevertheless seldom come close to it. In their own way, they must be happy.

I have a photograph of my mother and me standing on the balcony of a high-rise apartment we lived in at the time. I am wearing a school uniform. My mother has somehow procured an adult-sized version of the uniform and is standing next to me. We both wear a mournful expression, mine most visible in my eyes, open hugely wide and staring at the camera. My mother wears her sadness in the tightness of her lips, almost pursed in a look that says she is unsatisfied, that the world owes her more. Her eyes are settled, however, warm and forgiving.

The picture would have been taken sometime in the summer of 1976. It was the one time my father left the house for an extended period of time. He had departed in a hailstorm of yelling and doors slamming. Early pictures of them before my birth, or when I was still only a few years old, show a couple whose faces are relaxed. Usually the pictures are taken in the bedroom with me romping about on the floor. The weariness starts showing up years later.

He was gone for what may have been two weeks. A silence descended over the house. In the evenings, the light in the kitchen took on a yellow, shadowy twinge. The radio, normally blaring over all my parents' conversations, was never turned up to more than a sliver of sound. Children's books often have illustrations of archetypal winter cottages, the windows glazed with ice and snow, the heads of the people inside seen only by the light of a simple gas lamp. For those two weeks, I felt I was living inside one of those drawings. In some ways, it was peaceful. What had been a household constantly in turmoil, where discussions of politics were as rowdy as those over home economics, was not so magically transformed into a Norman

Rockwell painting. For once I had a normal, though admittedly one-parent, family. I recall feeling relaxed but also frightened, as if the silence had calmed my nerves but shocked my heart into subterfuge.

In the annals of divorce, my two-week almost experience would never qualify as a worthwhile case study. Studies tell me that in time my shellshock may have turned into anger, or would have led to life-long emotional reticence. Or not. What it did do is make me think about why it was merely an almost-divorce. I still don't have the answer: staying together for the kid probably had something to do with it.

My father came home one late afternoon. My mother told me to stay in my room while they talked out on the balcony. I hunched under my open window and listened to what they said — I have no idea what their words were; all I remember is scoring the conversation like a hockey announcer. Oh no, she made an accusation, he's getting mad, he's walking, oh, he's walking back now, he's apologizing, she's apologizing.

Eventually I was summoned to the balcony. Very formally, I was told that my parents had decided to stay together for my sake, because I would be unhappy if I came from a broken home. Whatever the reason, it seemed an all right outcome to me. Within a short enough time, the volume in the house rose again. We were dysfunctional but we were a "we."

I doubt the scenario would be repeated today, over two decades later. Leaving would not also include coming back. I've often wondered if the Eastern European culture where my parents grew up doesn't have something to do with their staying together. No more importance was placed on marriage in Romania than is placed in North America. Women worked outside the home, Romanian men do as little (or as much) housework as their Canadian or American counterparts. Except for one difference: the value of romantic love. Walk around most European cities on a warm fall or spring day and the number of couples holding hands, kissing, and just looking thrilled to be in each other's company, is far higher than in, say, Toronto. The strength of romantic hope is higher too. People expect more out of a relationship and out of each other. In the end, I think this accounts for my parents being together in spite of the odds. The simple power of romance — of the promise that marriage will be a blissful respite from the world — has maybe kept them going, attempting to reach for that impossibility.

The first time I read *Bridget Jones's Diary* was a year after it had come out. The vision of women it presented instantly repulsed me. I could see Bridget sitting by her phone, willing it to ring, counting her calories, smoking cigarette after cigarette in the never-ending silence, snatching up the receiver when it finally rang only to find one of her female buddies on the other line, hang up, and commence the whole process again. Bridget never read a book, never went to a movie by herself, just assuaged her loneliness by shopping or going to the pub with the gals.

While the book self-deprecatingly made light of Bridget's travails, it repelled me because underneath Helen Fielding's light touch lurked the darker truth. Every woman I knew at the time was only a few short steps away from living in Bridget's hell. All we had to do was give up all the things that kept us sane: the books, the talks, the walks, the movies, the interest in life outside of a partner, and the whole deck of cards would come tumbling down. We would all be revealed as lonely, hollow people, condemned to share Bridget's perpetual terror.

Compare her adventures to those of Dean Cassidy in Jack Kerouac's *On the Road*, a novel that defined a generation as exuberantly as Fielding has parsimoniously come to define hers. Kerouac felt compelled to chase after the ones burning like Roman candles; he thought they were the only people worth following. Juvenile, not burdened with responsibilities and with children and parents and even as something as simple as a job, Cassidy merrily romped around the United States. Having made his choice, the boy never complains. Bridget chose her life of diets and cigarettes and pubs too. So why do mornings find her hung-over and sniveling in a corner wondering will she be found surrounded by cats, or serve as a calorie-rich meal for an Alsatian?

I dislike Bridget so much because her life is what both women and men fear — pretending otherwise is the lie at the heart of liberal individualism. A woman without a man is not like a fish without a bicycle, a woman without a man, without a partner, is one very lonely human being. As is a man. If only loneliness and desperation could be as ecstatically written about as the lure of the road.

In January, after the lightshow and goodwill of the holidays, and stretching sometimes into the end of March, is the worst time to be single. There must have been other times, but I remember a month maybe a couple of years ago. It was probably the beginning of February. January that year had been particularly cold and unfriendly. Some days the heat in my apartment was unpredictable. I would crawl into bed in the evening and hide under layers of duvets and blankets. At three or four in the morning I'd wake up and feel strange, as if invisible bodies had entered my bedroom and were preventing me from having anyone I could hold in my bed, as if they were warding off love. Marriage is no cure for such a profound sense of exile. You cannot be with someone to keep from being alone, but when a marriage is good, it is also that: a defense against the ghosts who want to shatter our sleeping, vulnerable selves. As Aristotle said even before cities became the wastelands of human communion they can now be, "human beings are more naturally inclined to live in couples than in urban society."[88]

People surely get married for lots of reasons: because even now, in the dying days of patriarchy, some women look to some men for protection; because realistically, a double-income household is a far more viable economic unit than a single-income household; and yes, because sometimes they fall in love and it's what you do if you're in love and your parents keep asking when they're going to have grandchildren.

No one ever knows what happens inside a marriage. The pulling apart and the coming back together repeated over the course of months, then as time passes, years; sometimes long, wintry stretches are forgotten after a few short months of bliss or at least happiness. No one ever knows just how many times one must forget to continue a long marriage. In the 18th century, libertine Thomas Paine thought marriage by its very nature was doomed.

"As ecstasy abates, coolness succeeds which often makes way for indifference: and that for neglect: sure of each other by the nuptial bond, they no longer take any pains to be mutually agreeable; careless if they displease; and yet angry if reproached; with so little relish for each other's company, that anyone's else is welcome and more entertaining. Their union thus broke, they pursue separate pleasures; never meet but to wrangle, or part but to find comfort in other society."[89] Like Bertrand Russell's a couple of centuries later, Paine's solution was free love.

Others thought simple gestures could keep a marriage from disintegrating into Paine's farce. "Be devoted. Keep up your courtship," advises a 1899 manual for husbands. "Remember and repeat the little attentions which gave you pleasure months and years ago simply because you knew that they were a source of pleasure to the one whom you coveted as your bride and companion for life." The guide goes on to speak of women's work in words that may surprise those who say that women's work in the home has traditionally been devalued. "A woman is required to be everything. . . . Remember her days are long, just as busy, and more full of petty cares than yours. . . . Are you careful of your own appearance in the long evenings when there is no other woman but her to be captivated by your manly charms? I am inclined to believe that is more excuse for her . . . do not excuse your indifference and neglect of fond attentions, for they are just as dear to that careworn wife of yours at forty-five, or even fifty years as at twenty-two. . . . Your answer may be: 'My wife knows I love her, and that's enough.' She may know it, but it is a pleasant thing to be assured of now and then, and if there were more everyday assurances there would be fewer careless, heart-starved wives."[90]

I quote this at such length because it speaks to the estrangement that has bedeviled couples since time immemorial and also so simply about how to avoid it. To follow all this, for both parties, seems so very difficult.

Yet when we see a successful marriage it can make the rest of us take this quite unfathomable leap of faith. I read somewhere once a quip about how to look at one's wife or husband is to look death in the eye. Chilling, no? But flip the words around and they can mean that every time you sleep with your spouse, knowing (and hoping) that it will be until death parts you, it's a slap in the face of mortality. I'd say that that's why we persist in getting married — it's not that we refuse to accept that we may die before our spouse or that the person who will spend their life with us may very well die before us and leave us on our own for a good long time, it's that we accept the tragedy of that and indeed, embrace it. When the English philosopher and writer Iris Murdoch was ailing with Alzheimer's, novelist John Bayley, her husband for 40 years, looked after her.

"Rather than regarding her as a victim, incapable of sentience or emotional needs, John doted on Iris as if this were their honeymoon, and she his newly won bride. Like Orpheus, he acted as if he could do the impossible, and transport his beloved back from a dark underworld that had robbed her of her sanity,"[91] a friend of the couple said of visiting them. I think that's the poignancy of marriage, being able and prepared and willing to do that.

The trick, I think, is to remember that marriage is solace and refuge but also not only that, not always that. After the early bliss comes a lot of heartache, and then bliss again, perhaps this time stretched thinner and also deeper and more valuable for the passage of time. In his books about his wife's illness and death, Bayley wrote repeatedly of growing "closer apart" in his marriage as the years went on. It takes a profound love and profound understanding of the limitations of that love if it is to survive, to recognize the separateness integral to a successful marriage. I doubt anyone really gets it right.

Bayley's lesson to those in less extreme circumstances might be that a marriage is made up of trying to understand how to love. There's none of this tension — between the self and the other, the individual and the union — in the pages of *Bridget* (or the countless clones which have sprung up in her wake), or in the adventures of the single girls in *Sex & the City*. What we have instead are the likes of Laura Doyle, author of *The Surrendered Wife*, who sings the gospel of wives giving up control to their husbands. Don't nag, don't demand, don't criticize, don't tell him when he's taken the wrong turn on the highway, and presto, he'll help out around the house on his own and want to have sex more often too.[92] Or a $10,000 course called Marriage Works, which promises to teach women how to find an eligible husband and change their aura at the same time.[93]

I don't recognize yearning or loneliness in any of these roads to happiness, nor true joy or abandon, nor moments of real, true ugliness, or moments of quiet, shared peace. I don't recognize any of the things I wish for in the images that popular culture gives me. (I do occasionally recognize something of real-life in Ally McBeal, in the late-night walks she takes home at the end of each episode. Hokey as these walks invariably are, what with rain perennially falling on her head, she does seem to capture the feeling of searching for a place in her heart to call home.)

Some might accuse me of being a snob, a spoilsport, unable to take light pleasure in ogling the clothes on *Sex & the City*, or learning the recipes they use for cocktails, or how to decorate my house like theirs.

I think the truth is that I'm a dreamer. I want far, far more than what's being offered to me in the modern depictions of love and marriage. Why can we no longer have the dramatic personalities of Tolstoy's *War and Peace* and *Anna Karenina*, of the redeeming power of Raskolnikov's love for Sonya, the devotion of the *Song of Solomon* and the sadness and hidden ferocity of Ethan Allen Hawley. These books are all about married people — they're not a fraction as boring as the singletons in modern movies. With its imaginative poverty, popular culture can at best give us the biting specter of Elizabeth Taylor and Richard Burton, gnawing bits off each other's wounds in *Who's Afraid of Virginia Woolf*, or the modern equivalent, Kathleen Turner and Michael Douglas hanging off the chandelier and still trying to kill each other in *War of the Roses*. But the equivalent beauty, the stories that tell us what a *good* marriage looks like, are rare. The sun sets on Jane Austen's heroines when they marry. At the movies, it sets after the wedding.

There are some writers who express the trepidation marriage inspires, as well as the hopes, in modern, sparse words. In one of Stacey Richter's short stories, a single girl has decided her whole life is going to be spent solo. In order to make something out of her new reality, she submits a grant proposal for an art installation entitled The Cat Lady. The project is a document of her life as she ages, surrounded by cats. Then she meets her neighbor, who owns a pet rat. Immediately he acquires the moniker Rat Boy.

"I'm worried he might be dissolving something inside me that's very precious, very dear! He might be clogging up my urge to transform my life into a solitary artwork. I'm afraid he could possibly undermine the entire Cat Lady Project, and that the desire to give it up is already crouching within me. With a little prompting, I'm afraid I'd relinquish my work, and marry the Rat Boy, and move to the suburbs and become occupied with a plot of lawn and a baby or two." Rat Boy is wise. "Rat Boy insists it doesn't have to be like this. He says we can collaborate and that it would in fact be pretty cool; that conflict is an exciting part of being human creatures."[94]

"The unhappiest people I know, romantically speaking, are the ones who like pop music the most; and I don't know whether pop music has caused this unhappiness, but I do know that they've been listening to the sad songs longer than they've been living the unhappy lives,"[95] says Nick Hornby in *High Fidelity*, which was an unbelievably astute book before it became an OK movie and right at this moment, as I'm writing this, I'm listening to a Toronto radio station that is an especially egregious offender in this regard. All day, they play soft rock, melodies that alarm even as they soothe, that make me ponder whether anyone's love can ever measure up to the lyrics of the songs that colonize our minds. Do lovers really need a little time apart, do I want the kind of love where my eyes cry every night for someone. Maybe I really should just let it be. And that's just one 15-minute mix. My CD collection has somehow become populated with a group of broken-hearted singer/songwriters. When a fierce mood overtakes me, there's always Patti Smith, Ani Di Franco, or Hole, although as I get older, their unmediated fury comforts me less and less.

So if I think about marriage, most of what I prefer to go by is real-life. And whether my grandparents' marriage, my parents', some of my friends, or the conversations of my not-married friends, who wonder if they'll ever find someone they can foresee a life with, the reality is up for interpretation. We are all doomed to unhappy lives, or we all have the potential to create relationships that are often good enough, and sometimes much, much better than good enough.

It's not fashionable to pronounce that perhaps happiness can be found merely in the good enough, the fight not started, the dinner quietly enjoyed, the long, rambling walk in the fall. That no relationship can survive without the bouquets of flowers and the calls just to say I love you, but that those aren't every day things. To say that is to be traditional in a way, to harken back to a time when marriages endured despite disappointments and hurt, when a marriage like the one between Lev Tolstoy and his wife Sonya actually lasted. A raucous affair at the best of times, during its last years, the marriage truly unraveled. At 82, Tolstoy ran away from home and then barred his wife from his deathbed.[96] To say that something like this, much as I wouldn't wish it, is not inexplicable, that it still has value, is perhaps what pop psychologists would at best call settling. What would happen to Lev and Sonya today? An army of experts would be parachuted in, twice-weekly counseling sessions ordered. Wonderful as I think all these things are to help build an enduring union, they cannot alter the unstable nature of human temperaments, the winds of illness and ill fortune, or the unpredictability of life and how any one of us reacts under pressure.

On the other hand, some have a much lower tolerance for drama than either Lev or Sonya before declaring that they prefer peace to passion. In a *Harper's Bazaar* article, one wife says her only complaint was that her husband's sex drive was too high. "I'm very demanding, and he does his best to please me. He does the dishes. He makes money. He's good with the kids. He's got a sense of humor and an interesting mind. He used to be depressed, but now that he's on Prozac, he's not, and he's not horny either. What more could I want?"[97]

I don't like this anymore than Lev and Sonya's story, but both cases are instructive. If we're to move any closer to understanding what marriage requires and what it doesn't, shouldn't our pop culture and pop psychologists — after all, pop's what most of us get most of our info from — give us more of these scenes from mixed-up marriages, of the ones that endure despite the faltering. Only by knowing where others have failed, will we be able to be easier on our own failures.

In the course of writing a first draft of this chapter, I happened on a book about marriage at the used bookshop in my neighborhood. Thrilled by the serendipity, I picked it up hoping for something unexpected that had maybe been placed there just for me to find, a new insight. A half-hour later, I was still immersed in the book. Supposedly an analysis of men and marriage, it was yet another entry in the catalogue of books aimed at women wanting to "catch" a mate. Playing hard to get is advised, the emotional reticence of men knowingly frowned upon, and frequent nods given to the importance to being independent. Marriage in this formulation is just an extension of dating — which means, of course, that it follows many of the same strategies. Keep him hungry and he'll stay keen. Should problems crop up refer to page 101, bottom paragraph.

I cannot imagine that anyone would be able to keep up this kind of farce in a real-life marriage without resorting to Prozac. I imagine that the majority of unions based on this kind of deception (I am never needy, tearful, worried, anxious or plain irrational) cannot last.

Much as women might desire marriage, we are also conscious of not making the kinds of choices that we think led to the doom of women who came before us. Ironically, the reputation of marriage is falling just as the situation for women choosing to marry is improving. In 1700, a woman might reasonably expect in Mary Astell's words of the time "to be yok'd for life to a disagreeable person and temper; to have folly and ignorance tyrannize over wit and sense; to be contradicted in every thing one does or says, and bore down not by reason but the will and pleasure of an absolute Lord and Master, whose commands she cannot but despise at the same time she obeys them." Not surprisingly, Astell added "[it] is a misery none can have a just idea of, but those who have felt it."[98]

Accomplished women are not free of being yoked. Recently much has been made of women who, it is said, would have been better off looking after themselves with the same degree of care and understanding they lavished on their husbands. The wives of the writers and editors who worked at the New York-based political and literary journal *The Partisan Review* in the thirties, forties and fifties were a spectacular bunch, among them Mary McCarthy and Diana Trilling. Both are clever, witty, socially penetrating writers in their own right, with their own body of work. But part of their self-worth, as writer Stacy Schiff explains, came from their private life. These were women who wanted to be as "remembered for [their] wit as for [their] blueberry pancakes."[99]

History is littered with women like these. Women with prodigious talents of their own who don't put all their eggs in their own basket, but instead channel some, or even all, of their life into that of their husbands'. Schiff, who also wrote a biography of Vera Nabokov, tells of Vera typing all of Vladimir's hand-written manuscripts, organizing his date book, answering his correspondence and attending his lectures as his most faithful student. (At one point in their marriage, she paraded in front of the Montreaux hotel they called home with a sign which read: "more money for auxiliary services.") Yet Nabokov was attracted to the Russian beauty not because of her skills as a secretary, but because of her sex appeal. On first meeting him, she wore a mask designed to capture the handsome young man's interest. What would Vera have amounted to had she devoted that same energy to her own career? For feminists, she symbolizes all that a woman can do wrong.

The truth might be trickier, as Schiff suggests. Possibly Vera would not have amounted to much of anything at all, at best a provincial wife chafing at life with a bureaucrat husband. Not everyone is cut out to conquer the world or finds fulfillment in being at the top of the mountain. Vera was uniquely talented at loving her husband.

Simone de Beauvoir served the same function for Jean-Paul Sartre that Vera served for Nabokov, except her reasons are much more difficult to fathom. Every day she sat in the Café des Flores after he'd dumped another of his manuscripts on her lap to edit while he ran off to chase Parisian skirt. Meanwhile, she was sharpening her claws and writing *The Second Sex*, a condemnation of women who lived through their husbands. At least those women were getting something more tangible in return than mere words. De Beauvoir truly frightens me, a powerhouse of a woman who somehow did not have the strength to face her own needs and emotions. She never did come to terms with her role in Sartre's life, carrying on a 30-year affair with writer Nelson Algren, but never being able to break free of her platonic marriage.

After how many years, Sartre lying on his deathbed in the hospital, takes her wrist. "I love you very much, my dear Castor [he called her the Beaver, a nickname of hers from university]," de Beauvoir recalls him saying in *Adieux*, her account of her life with Sartre. "On April 14 he was asleep when I came; he woke and said a few words without opening his eyes, then he held up his lips to me. I kissed his mouth and cheek. These words and these actions were unusual for him; they were obviously related to the prospect of his death."[100]

It wasn't just famous women who suffered silently. For many years, my mother and I would talk at the kitchen table after I came home from school. The stories changed, but the tenor of them did not. A lot of them were about her own mother, who died before I was born. A beauty with translucent skin, blue eyes, and dark hair, she married a writer and art critic. Before the marriage, she was a children's short story writer. Only a couple of them were ever published but they are preserved in a plastic folder in one of my mother's boxes of papers. After the marriage, she had two children in fairly quick succession. Her husband increasingly neglected her, stayed out late with his friends, drinking and discussing art and politics with other writers and the students who took his classes and worshipped their professor. Fights ensued, of course, with my grandfather taking the predictable course of spending more and more time away from the wife who had become the source of his grief.

In summer, my grandmother would take my mother and her brother on holiday. Her husband would join her, supposedly for the whole summer. He rarely stayed more than two weeks before hightailing it back to the city. That would have been the fifties, the decade of the stay-at-home mom. The options she would have had would not have been as apparent to her, and the social pressure to stay together much higher than now.

Women today hold the men in our intimate lives to much higher standards than our mothers and grandmothers did. At a panel on feminism in New York in 1999, one woman in the audience told the assembled leading lights (Gloria Steinem, bell hooks, Diane Ackerman, and others) that what she really wanted in a man was someone who was fully dedicated to her career. "You want a wife," Steinem said. "Yes!" the woman exclaimed. Few women are so unburdened by society's expectations that they can happily tell their friends that their husbands are housewives. I have to say that this model has always made more sense to me than the current two harried, career-obsessed people attempting to find a moment for themselves, or for each other. We don't stay home and mix cocktails for 6 o'clock. Nor would we want to. But we also don't necessarily want to just go to work and come home to have cocktails mixed for us. What we want I think is someone who is sort of like a wife, but happy about it, someone busy with their own work but not so busy as to be unable to take a load off for us.

Another nightmare no young woman tires of talking about is what I call the "dishes" nightmare. You'd think feminism had done its work at least in this area, but save for a few, selected men who take women's studies courses as much to pick up girls as to deepen their historical knowledge, this one constant seems most impervious to change. Roughly sketched, it goes like this: Once upon a time, a woman was young, beautiful, and desirable. The man who fell in love with her did not do so because she was really good at doing the dishes (or vacuuming, or picking up his socks, or newspapers). Yet unbelievably, sometimes within a matter of months, she's doing the dishes; her sensuality surely on its way to sudden death. His will shortly follow. Every woman rebels at doing housework not just because she's far too busy for it, but also because it transforms her from a pretty girl to the man's mother.

No wonder a dating relationship now is likely to be conducted as a job interview. Not everyone is looking for marriage, perhaps they're merely looking for a long-term relationship, someone to spend time, a lot of it, with. What is amusing about the job interview dating life is that it is made possible by the illusion that we live forever. No one wants to spend her life shackled to another human being if someone else is out there waiting to offer them perfect happiness, or at least more of a quotient of it. In the 12th century, say, a man who married a young lass could expect to be responsible for her for maybe ten years, until she eventually died in childbirth. The number of years we have to live in relative companionable peace these days with the same person has risen to as high as 50, or if we marry early, 60 years. 60 years!

Part of the trepidation to marriage in the West comes from another source, particularly for women around my age. Some of us aren't terribly sure we would be much good at it. We're lippy, full of attitude, able to look after ourselves financially and with enough friends to be sure that should we reach a ripe old age in singledom we can always move in with each other for companionship. And as one of my friends cheerfully advises, and another friend warns, raise cats. We would all like to have sex every single night, but we also know that won't be the case and that wish is also tempered by the fervent desire of never seeing ourselves scrubbing the kitchen floor while our spouse drinks beer on the couch.

"[Women] who had the good fortune to grow up cherished by their parents . . . [won't exchange] a father, a man who despite the blinkers of his upbringing had come, painfully and triumphantly, to accept this swirling, sassy maelstrom whom he once called his little girl as real . . . for a husband who hadn't learnt anything about women at all because he thought he knew everything already," writes Julie Burchill in her novel *Married Alive*. "I'll tell you a thing, and it's a terrible thing. I know for sure that my generation of women fake orgasms with men so much more than our mothers did. Fake everything. Love, laughter, happy ever after."[101]

It doesn't get any worse than that and I don't want any part of this picture.

All this wisdom we have acquired has come at a price. For a generation that came of age against a backdrop of horror stories, high divorce rates, and melded families with stepmothers and stepfathers all playing a part, the responses have varied. We either fight very hard to keep what we have, to improve its texture enough so that we can live with it, or we can give up very quickly. What we all have in common are much higher levels of conflict between partners. We may be more willing to struggle to achieve romance — a seeming paradox. No one my age, however, thinks or expects a romance to proceed effortlessly. The rules of romance have changed. What once was set in stone, the cracks visible only after marriage, is now visible before. We no longer have codes of courtship and without those, our roles in marriage have changed as well.

Every Sunday, the *New York Times* runs marriage announcements. Placed by well-off families, the notices of nuptials could well have been written one or two centuries ago. Between the lines lie the social machinations, the striving toward joining a better class, the search to find someone who one is not only romantically attracted to, but also fulfills one's spoken and unspoken contractual expectations. For some time, I was addicted to looking at the announcements, the people named in them characters in a drama of mini-Shakespearean dimensions.

Liberals look at the concept of arranged marriages with eyes jaundiced by our attachment to the idea of romantic love. To marry someone whom you have not picked yourself as your heart's only desire seems anathema to every word in every sonnet or rock song ever composed. Arranged marriages imply that love can be made to develop; given two people who are somewhat compatible in temperament and interests, the spontaneous magic doesn't have to be so spontaneous after all. Yet when you read the *NYT* nuptial announcements it becomes clear that the best and brightest among us do nothing so different than what is practiced in arranged marriages.

The good-looking, talented, and wealthy (or potentially wealthy) pick people similarly situated who will help them in their life. Romantic love aside, everyone still tries to make the best match they can. Jane Austen's heroines never married for love alone, but also for money. Love alone could not guarantee a long lasting marriage — for that you needed finances. It's always been thus, really. You can only sell your hair to buy a watchstrap, your watchstrap to buy a comb, for so many Christmases before the reality of your situation becomes oppressive.

I never did quite understand why all the fuss was made over *Who Wants to Marry a Millionaire?*, the Fox-TV show that sold off a bride to a supposed millionaire. People assess a potential partner's earnings versus their own needs and expectations every day. And some, both men and women, don't make the cut. Others have to sign prenuptial agreements. Perhaps knowing that you need a big house, a couple of SUVs and twice-yearly tropical holidays to keep your marriage happy makes you shallow. Perhaps it just makes you realistic and self-aware. Perhaps you don't care about money and think you can live on idealism and love alone, but even that is a choice that required thinking about money at some point.

Other times, in other cultures, the solution to the problem of marriage was for the parents of the bride and groom to arrange such a union. Even stripped of the negative implications — at their worst, arranged marriages can be just the selling of the family's daughters to the highest bidder — such arrangements are still deficient in Western eyes.

In university, some seven years ago, I had a friend who was to be wed in an arranged marriage. Her parents forbade her to date, and although she had male friends and men who were interested in her, no potential relationship stood a chance. Her betrothed was already a successful man, a few years older. In his presence, she was shy and giggly.

"Do you think he's cute? What do you think?" I remember her asking one day in the spring the day when we first met him. Some of her friends had been invited by her family to visit her home and meet the man. The practice appeared somewhat antiquated to us. He was calling on her. With us white kids we only brought someone home if we felt like it, if it looked like they might stick around for a while. Funnily enough, for Naheen, the sentiment was not dissimilar. To meet one's friends and family is saying that this person who dropped from the sky last week is going to play a part in our lives, but it also warns the partner that others are looking out for our welfare: that they are accountable not just to us but to the community. Arranged marriages just make all this transparent. Once my friend's community had given its approval, however, it also left the couple alone. In the end, the two were divorced. The man who had seemed liberated before marriage was said to have turned into a tyrant of sorts after. I didn't keep in touch with her which I am still sorry for and so don't know the details of how the story ended.

The impending nuptials, however, caused as much havoc among her friends as must have been in her heart. This was the early 90s, the days when so-called political correctness was casting its spell over university campuses. Any family that would give their daughter to a man she did not already love clearly belonged to another era. To save the woman from this marriage was tantamount to making a huge step forward for feminism. Here she was, talented, determined, already a trail-blazer, a girl from a traditional family who lied and said she was studying at the library so that she could work on the campus radio station. She had so many options, her white female friends kept telling her. She could stand up to her family, turn away from centuries of tradition and carve her own way in the world, one day find her own man.

I didn't say much about it, though I asked if she was all right with the decision, asked about her family. To this day, I don't know if any of us were right in our actions. Did I not counsel against the marriage because as an immigrant daughter myself I could identify with the pressure she was under from her tight-knit family? Did I not do so simply because I was too busy with my own life to give her more time and cloaked my sympathy in the mantle of cultural non-interference? Or did I not do so because I thought a measured out love might have as good a chance of success as a marriage based on *amour fou*? What if someone had presented me with a man when I was 18 or 20 or 22, a hypothetical me that had never been in love with anyone else, and told me that I would be spending the rest of my days with them for better or worse? I don't know if my heart could embrace them, but I don't know what my heart would look like either if it had never found its own rhythm to keep time by. I don't know if our hearts are even always right; perhaps I kept quiet with my friend because I thought marriage is always a risky proposition, an arranged one having different perils than one based on love, but both potentially dangerous to one's sanity, health, and resilience.

We place such a high premium on free will, though, that the idea of not being the ones doing the choosing strikes most of us as repulsive. The results are not stellar. As Bertrand Russell wrote, somewhat nastily, marriage based primarily on romantic love is an illusion. "Each imagines the other to be possessed of more than mortal perfections, and conceives that marriage is going to be one long dream of bliss. . . . In America, where the romantic view of marriage has been taken more seriously than anywhere else, and where law and custom alike are based upon the dreams of spinsters, the result has been an extreme prevalence of divorce and an extreme rarity of happy marriages."[102] Romantic love has been linked to marriage only in recent history. The grand passions of courtly love, such as the one on which the legends of Lancelot and Guinevere and Tristan and Isolde are based, are doomed forms of love. These stories end in death not just because it's romantic that way, but because the romances that have captivated our hearts since they entered the record of human stories would captivate us less if they ended with Lancelot and Guinevere fighting about who is master of the remote control.

Marriage has always demanded compromises — otherwise it's an untenable proposition. These days no one wants to admit they are making compromises; every problem is seen as a potential cause for termination. Like the marketplace, marriage has become a battlefield. Nineteenth-century men felt a conflict between the competitive demands of the workplace and the emotional demands of the home. In one they were expected to be hard, in another soft. Now both partners have split personalities. Women today are much better at looking out for ourselves than our mothers, but I'm not convinced we are better at love. The birth control pill is said to have liberated men to chase after the milk and not the cow, but in the long-term it has also made the cow less likely to give herself to the first, second, third, or fourth man who's interested in more than the milk.

Man or woman, we yearn for nothing more or less than what Portia described to her husband Brutus in *Julius Caesar.* Seeing him preoccupied, Portia basically tells Brutus to not shut her out. "Am I yourself / But, as it were, in sort or limitation; / To keep with you at meals, comfort your bed, / And talk to you sometimes? Dwell I but in the suburbs / Of your good pleasure? / If it be no more, Portia is Brutus's harlot, not his wife."[103] We want to be lover and confidante, playmate, dinner mate and adviser to spouses, to play a role we can play for no one else, kings and queens of one land.

In the meantime, of course, daily life interferes. We do not spend our days pondering mortality while washing the kids' clothes or having an after-work drink with the significant other. If we did, we would miss the journey, the road for the destination. Ultimately, it's the journey that I find fascinating, especially these days. When culture is exploding with sexual kinks, when the covers of women's magazines like *Cosmopolitan* still blare "How to keep your man intrigued" and they're talking about one's husband, when bed death is a never-ending topic, how do people really keep from getting divorced?

A couple who have somehow managed to keep that spark of passion alive for 40 years, may look at each other and be turned on at the same time, for much the same reasons. They have been together for so long that they truly love each other. For the woman, though, that love is likely to be mixed with toleration, compassion, and affection. A man will look at his wife of 40 years, he will look at how old she has become, how the skin on her body sags and she's losing her hair and maybe where her breasts used to be round and firm they are now dry and sagging too, and then he will find that pocket of conventional beauty, that beauty mark he remembers first seeing above her lip and he will feel lust.

I would like to think that my grandparents weren't so far from this image. My grandfather would look at my grandmother and he would turn to me and say: "Look at her, isn't she pretty?" I'd nod, though in reality she was no longer a great beauty. It didn't matter. My grandmother would laugh, scold him, rub his back and then tell him he was a fool. Would that my desires turn into this.

NOTES

[1]Regine Deforges, *Confessions of O*, (New York: The Viking Press, 1979), p.51
[2]Lisa Palac, *The Edge of the Bed: How Dirty Pictures Changed My Life* (Boston: Little Brown, 1998), p. 8.
[3]Carson McCullers, *The Ballad of The Sad Café and Other Stories* (New York: Bantam Books, 1962), p. 1.
[4]Sharon Olds, *The Sign of Saturn* (London: Secker & Warburg, 1999), p. 70.
[5]Jean Genet, *Miracle of the Rose* (New York: Grove Press, 1966), p. 90.
[6]Peter B. Anderson, Cindy Struckman-Johnson, Cynthia Struckman-Johnson, eds., *Sexually Aggressive Women* (New York: Guilford Press, 1998).
[7]Rachel P. Maines, *The Technology of Orgasm: "Hysteria," the Vibrator, and Women's Sexual Satisfaction* (Baltimore: Johns Hopkins University Press, 1999).
[8]Wendy Shalit, *A Return to Modesty: Discovering the Lost Virtue* (New York: Free Press, 1999), p. 169.
[9]Naomi Wolf, *Promiscuities: The Secret Struggle for Womanhood* (New York: Random House, 1997), pp. 217–20.
[10]Simone de Beauvoir, *The Second Sex*, (New York: Vintage Books, 1989), p. 655.
[11]Anais Nin, *Delta of Venus*, (London: Book Club Associates,), p. 115.
[12]Peter Lehman, *Running Scared: Masculinity and the Representation of the Male Body* (Philadelphia: Temple University Press, 1993), p. 146.
[13]Ibid., p. 150.
[14]Stephen Boyd, ed., *Life Class: The Academic Male Nude 1820–1920*. (London: Gay Men's Press, 1989), p. 10.
[15]Susan Faludi, *Stiffed: The Betrayal of the American Man* (New York: W. Morrow and Co., 1999), p. 499.
[16]Lehman, p. 166.
[17]*The Independent*, "News of the Weird", April 27, 1998.
[18]Maureen Tisdale, "Battling a Bad Reputation," in *Florida Today*, Nov. 10, 1999.

[19]Beth Bailey, *From Front Porch to Back Seat: Courtship in Twentieth-Century America* (Baltimore: Johns Hopkins University Press, 1998), p. 89.
[20]Deuteronomy 22:20–22.
[21]Françoise Barret-Ducrocq (translated by John Howe), *Love in the Time of Victoria: Sexuality, Class and Gender in Nineteenth-Century London* (London, New York: Verso, 1991), p. 23.
[22]Ibid., p. 21
[23]Bridget Hill, ed., *Eighteenth-Century Women: An Anthology* (London, Boston: Allen & Unwin, 1984), p. 31.
[24]Peggy Orenstein, *Schoolgirls: Young Women, Self-Esteem and the Confidence Gap* (New York: Doubleday, 1994), p. 63.
[25]Charmaine Chan interviews Annabel Chong, *South China Morning Post*, April 8, 2000.
[26]"Ruffling More Than Sheets" (interview with Annabel Chong), *The Korea Herald*, May 5, 2000.
[27]Bailey, p. 93.
[28]Quoted in Wolf, p. 145. When Princess Maria Theresa asked her physician why, though married, she was not pregnant, she was told: "I think the vulva of Her Most Holy Majesty should be titillated before intercourse."
[29]Ibid., p. 148.
[30]Ibid., p. 150.
[31]Ibid., p. 152.
[32]Marcelle Karp, Debbie Stoller, eds., *The Bust Guide to the New World Order* (New York: Penguin, 1999), pp. 102–03.
[33]Palac, p. 41.
[34]John Carlin, "A Woman of Little Importance," in *The Independent*, June 22, 1997.
[35]Leora Tanenbaum, *Slut! Growing Up Female with a Bad Reputation* (New York: Seven Stories Press, 1999), p. 101.
[36]Ira Tattleman, "Speaking to the Gay Bathhouse: Communicating in Sexually Charged Spaces," in *PublicSex/gay space*, William Leap, ed. (New York: Columbia University Press, 1999), p. 33.
[37]Leo Bersani, "Is the Rectum a Grave?" in *AIDS: Cultural Analysis, Cultural Activism*, Douglas Crimp, ed. (Cambridge: MIT Press, 1988), pp. 197–222.
[38]Tattleman, p. 83.
[39]Daniel Reitz, "I Hate Myself," in *Salon*, Sept. 14, 1999.
[40]Orenstein, p. 55.
[41]Tattleman, p. 55.
[42]Allan Berube, "The History of Gay Bathhouses," in *Policing Public Sex: Queer Politics and the Future of AIDS Activism*, Dangerous Bedfellows, eds. (Boston: South End Press, 1990), p. 202.
[43]Mitchel Raphael, "Divine Miss T as Divine Miss M at Bathhouse," in *National Post*, Aug. 26, 1999.
[44]Berube, p. 205.
[45]"Committee Resolves to Close Baths," in *My American History: Lesbian and Gay Life during the Reagan/Bush Years*, Sarah Schulman (New York:

Routlege, 1994), p. 115.
[46]"Health or Homophobia? Responses to the Bathhouse Guidelines"; and "Koch Ready to Close More Bathhouses" in *My American History*, Schulman.
[47]Deuteronomy 22:5.
[48]John Gregory Dunne, "The Humboldt Murders," in *The New Yorker*, Jan. 13, 1997.
[49]Dinitia Smith, *The Illusionist* (New York: Scribner, 1997), p. 209.
[50] *The Last Sex: Feminism and Outlaw Bodies*, Arthur and Marilouise Kroker, eds. (New York: St. Martin's Press, 1993), p. 113.
[51]Rudolf Dekker, *The Tradition of Female Transvestism in Early Modern Europe* (Houndmills: MacMillan Press, 1989), p. 68.
[52]Diane Wood Middlebrook, *Suits Me: The Double of Billy Tipton* (Boston: Houghton Mifflin, 1998), p. 68.
[53]"A Statement from Michigan Womyn's Music Festival," in *Off our Backs*, Jan. 10, 1999.
[54]Lillian Faderman, *Odd Girls and Twilight Lovers: A History of Lesbian Life in Twentieth-Century America* (New York: Columbia University Press, 1991.)
[55]Kroker, p. 110.
[56]Edmund White, *Genet: A Biography* (New York: Alfred A. Knopf, 1993), p. 273.
[57]Patricia Gagne and Richard Tewksbury, "Conformity Pressures and Gender Resistance Among Transgendered Individuals," in *Social Problems*, Feb. 1998.
[58]Kathleen Ann Lahey, *Are We Persons Yet?: Law and Sexuality in Canada* (Toronto: University of Toronto Press, 1999), p. 24.
[59]Ibid., p. 95.
[60]Holly Devor, *FTM: Female-to-Male Transsexuals in Society* (Bloomington: Indiana University Press, 1993), p. 450.
[61]Stephanie Nolen, "The Third Way," in *The Globe and Mail*, Sept. 25, 1999.
[62]Margaret Wente, "How David Found His Manhood," in *The Globe and Mail*, Jan. 29, 2000.
[63]Leslie Feinberg, *Transgender Warriors: Making History from Joan of Arc to RuPaul* (Boston: Beacon Press, 1996), p. 23.
[64]Jay Prosser, *Second Skins: A Gender and Culture Reader* (New York: Columbia University Press, 1998), pp. 232–33.
[65]Kroker, p. 111.
[66]Julian Dibbell, Mother Fixation, *Artbyte*, Nov/Dec 2000.
[67]A.L. Kennedy, "Loving Cuff," in *Nerve*, Dec. 9, 1999.
[68]"Dialogue with a Dominatrix," in *Women and Prostitution*, Vern L. Bullough, ed. (Buffalo: Prometheus Books, 1987), p. 80.
[69]Freud, p. 183.
[70]Thomas E. Murray, *The Language of Sadomasochism: A Glossary and Linguistic Analysis* (New York: Greenwood Press, 1989), p. 10.
[71]Ibid., p. 14.
[72]Ibid., p. 15.
[73]"Juliette, Juliette: Autobiography of a Dominatrix," in *Selves S&M Identities*, p. 91.

[74]Regine Deforges, *Confessions of O: Conversations with Pauline Reage* (New York: Viking Press, 1979), p. 10.
[75]Ibid., p. 9.
[76]Annalee Newitz, "Whip Me, Spank Me, Gentrify Me," in *Salon*, Jan. 15, 2000.
[77]Julia Gracen, "Chain Gang" in *Salon*, May 18, 2000.
[78]Molly Weatherfield, "The Mother of Masochism," in *Salon*, Aug. 6, 1998.
[79]Deforges, p. 114.
[80]Leah McLaren, "When the Girls Invade the Boys' Club," *The Globe and Mail*, July 31, 1999.
[81]Patrick J. Kiger, "Snorkeling in the Cesspool," *Los Angeles Times Magazine*, August 20, 2000.
[82]Susie Bright, *Susie Bright's Sexual State of the Union*, (New York: Simon & Schuster, 1997), p. 81.
[83]*Gizmotude Quotation Archives*, gizmotude. www5.50megs.com/ archive_marriage.com.
[84]A.M. Homes, *Music for Torching* (New York: Rob Weisbach Books, 1999), p. 53.
[85]Larissa Phillips, "The Case Against Matrimony," in *Salon*, Nov. 18, 1999.
[86]Katha Pollitt, *The Nation*, Oct. 23, 2000, p. 10.
[87]Robert Flaciere, *Love in Ancient Greece*, translated from the French by James Cleugh (New York: MacFadden, 1964), p. 107.
[88]Ibid., p. 15.
[89]Hill, p. 96.
[90]Sylvanus Stall, *What a Young Husband Ought to Know* (Philadelphia: Vir Pub. Co., 1907), p. 59.
[91]Robert Weil, "Memories of Iris," in *Partisan Review*, Sept. 10, 1999.
[92]Patrice Apodaca, "Let Him Drive," in *Los Angeles Times*, July 7, 1999.
[93]Liza Cooperman, "A Six-Month Plan to Find the Perfect Husband," in *National Post*, February 20, 2000.
[94]Stacey Richter, *My Date With Satan* (New York: Scribner, 1999), pp. 127–28.
[95]Nick Hornby, *High Fidelity* (New York: Riverhead Books, 1996), p. 25.
[96]Smoluchowski, Louise, *Lev and Sonya: The Story of the Tolstoy Marriage* (New York: Putnam, 1987).
[97]Susan Squire, "The Ideal Husband," in *Harper's Bazaar*, June 1997.
[98]Hill, p. 93.
[99]Stacy Schiff, "The Group," in *The New York Times Book Review*, Jan. 23, 2000.
[100]Simone de Beauvoir, *Adieux: A Farewell to Sartre,* translated by Patrick O'Brian (New York: Pantheon Books,1984), pp. 124–25.
[101]Julie Burchill, *Married Alive* (New York: Orion Books, 1999), p. 189.
[102]Bertrand Russell, *Marriage and Morals* (New York: Liveright, 1929), p. 51.
[103]William Shakespeare, *Julius Caesar*, in *The Complete Works of William Shakespeare* (New York: Avenel Books, 1980), p. 822.